What's
Self-Love
Got to do
With It?

What's Self-Love Got To Do With It? Copyright @ 2018 Heather Andrews

www.heatherandrews.press
www.followitthru.com

Compiled by Heather Andrews:
www.heatherandrews.press
www.followitthru.com

Book cover design by Lorraine Shulba: www.bluebugstudios.com

Editing by Suzanne LaVoie and Zoey Duncan:
www.suzannelavoiewrites.com
https://zoeyduncan.wordpress.com/

Copy editing manuscript compilation by Amanda: www.letsgetbooked.com

Proofreading by Abbie: http://pilcrowproofreading.co.uk/

Formatting by Bojan Kratofil: https://www.expertformatting.com/

ISBN: 978-1-5136-3625-2

Gratitude

Gratitude was something we practiced as a child growing up when it was Thanksgiving or Christmas. I was thankful for my parents, my family, and the life I had. However, I never really knew how blessed I was until I left home and had to deal with life on my own.

Who knew gratitude would become a daily practice in my life, that I would journal about all the blessings and why I am thankful for them?

In my journey as an entrepreneur, which started three years ago, I have come to learn that life is better when approaching it from a true state of love and gratitude. I am grateful for the opportunities that have come into my life and all the wonderful friends, relationships, authors and mentors I have met along the way.

Each of them has played a role that has been a blessing and essential to my growth as a human being.

That is the power of connection and love. That brings us to the reason for my creating this book. The world is a busy place, full of distractions that can test our belief in our self-worth. I connected to these amazing co-authors who have shared their heartfelt stories of how important it is to believe in the power of self and being open to learning the strategies to move through life's journey with openness, kindness, and support.

I am grateful they shared my passion for creating a book that would reach all generations. They shared a piece of their heart and soul with our readers to inspire and provide love from the pages of a book.

I am grateful for my mom who has modeled the way of love. She is a pillar of strength and always supported me.

I am grateful for my loving husband, he is my rock and advisor, and my kids who show me support and love daily.

Thank you to my publishing and marketing teams. I would be lost without your support and long hours of work. May we continue to soar to new heights together.

You each mean the world to me.

Thank you to my media production team at Tenacious Living Network, who keep the audiobooks and podcasts moving forward.

Lastly, to my co-authors who believed in themselves and shared their stories for the world to read, thank you from the bottom of my heart.

What's self-love got to do with it? Well…everything.

Enjoy your time with us.

Heather

Table of Contents

Foreword

Hi, my name is Erin, and I am a recovering perfectionist. (This is where you say, "Hi, Erin!".) For many, many years I masked my fear of not being good enough with performing, proving, and perfecting. I got the grades and degrees. I got the body. I won the awards. I excelled. I achieved. I tried to 'prove' my worth—and it early destroyed me. I was riddled with anxiety, a sense of never fitting in, and an extreme discomfort of being in my own skin.

I look back on those painful years and realize I had what I call a 'God-sized hole in my soul' that I attempted to fill with worldly accomplishments, victories, and other self-destructive behaviors —anything to make the pain go away.

My lack of self-love eventually led to depression and a 'dark night of the soul'. I was emotionally bankrupt. My cup was empty.

It was during my emotional rock bottom that I found the gym. Yep, the gym. I decided to start taking care of myself. What started out as a physical transformation moved into a spiritual and emotional transformation. I started taking risks, being myself, sharing my true thoughts and making mistakes, and I loved it! I had joined the human race. I finally felt like I belonged.

Through my weakness I found strength. Through my vulnerability I found power. Through my imperfection, I found beauty and strength.

The relationships that I had always wanted appeared in my life because I was learning to connect on an authentic and deep level. I fell in love with stepping outside of my comfort zone and in doing so, my perfectionism lost its oxygen supply. I learned that the best way to serve others is to first serve yourself. Not in a selfish way, but a self-'full' way.

One of my favorite thought leaders, Iyanla Vanzant, once said to Oprah, "How you treat yourself is how you treat God. Because YOU are the representative of God in your life. In your life, you've got to be as good to you as you want to be to God in order to be of service to others in the world."

Self-love truly is a win-win. It's not selfish to put yourself first. To be the best version of yourself is the most loving thing you can do, for yourself and for others. What comes out of the cup is for others but what is in the cup is yours, and it's your job to keep your cup full.

"I fully and completely love, accept, and approve of myself." If you were to rate how true this statement is for you with ten being, "Oh yes! This is exactly how I feel," and one being, "Ha-ha! No way! I don't believe that at all!" what number would you assign yourself?

Psychological research shows that a person's level of self-worth is highly correlated with their level of success, happiness, and joy. The higher their self-worth, the higher their success, happiness, and joy.

As a psychologist treating clients for the past sixteen years, the common factor that all of my clients share is emotional pain. Psychologists and the majority of all great philosophers in the world would agree that the etiology, the cause of human suffering and pain stems from a lack of knowing, and often a forgetting, of one's worth.

So why does self-worth allude so many of us? Why do so many of us struggle with knowing our inherent worth and value?

I have good news and bad news. The good news is that bliss is our birthright. The bad news is that we often forget. Thankfully, the stories in this book will help you remember! They will help you un-learn any 'bad' learning, lies, false teachings or incorrect messages you have received that have contributed to your lack of confidence or self-love.

As a psychologist and success coach, let me share with you my top strategies for increasing your self-love and in turn, your success:

1. **Behave your way into different thinking, instead of trying to think your way into different behaving.**

   Example: If you lack the confidence to be a public speaker, instead of trying to convince yourself you are a great speaker, you could hire a speaking coach, prepare, and then deliver your speech. In doing so, you will most likely receive positive feedback from others, realize that you did better than expected, and maybe even have some fun in the process. Your confidence will increase after you act—even while being afraid.

2. **Behave in ways that are consistent with your stated values.**

   Example: If being healthy and fit are goals and values of yours, but you treat yourself poorly by eating junk food and never exercising, it is going to be a tall order to feel great about yourself. What if you treated your body 'as if' you cared for it and fed it nutritious foods and moved it regularly? You would be behaving in line with your stated values. When you do that, you have a much higher chance of liking yourself. It really is as simple, and profound, as that. Keep those goals and values at the front and center of your mind. Remind yourself of them daily as they will continue to motivate you to act 'as if' you love yourself.

3. **Start using positive affirmations that work.**

    Example: Instead of staring at yourself in the mirror and saying a big fat lie, such as "I love everything about myself," try this three-step practice to change your 'stinking thinking' to more positive, healthy thinking.

    a. **Validate:** Ask yourself, "Why does it make perfect sense I am feeling this way?" This will help you validate where you learned to doubt yourself or maybe where some past learning experiences have taught you to think negatively. Maybe, for example, when you were a child someone told you that you weren't smart or would never amount to anything. Acknowledge that you learned to think this way about yourself, and say, "It makes perfect sense I don't think I'm smart enough because I was told that as a young, impressionable child."

    b. **Pivot:** This is the step where you choose to think differently, and it is as simple as saying to yourself, "I am capable of thinking differently and more positively about myself," or "I am learning to more fully and completely love and approve of myself."

    c. **Replace:** The last step is replacing your old, negative belief with a new, positive belief. Now, this is where things get tricky. Don't tell yourself a lie here. Don't say, "I am the smartest person on the planet." Instead, remind yourself you are open to change, growth, and learning to view yourself differently. Maybe you start with a statement such as, "I am learning to notice my strengths, and I continue to improve myself," or "I am growing every day and am open to loving myself more every day."

The stories in this book are just like yours. It is our humanity that is our common bond.

Be inspired as you learn how these authors rose out of the ashes of self-doubt, low self-esteem, and fear, and stepped into their greatness and personal power. Remember, when one person shines his or her light, it gives others permission to shine theirs. So, shine on.

With love,
Dr. Erin Oksol
http://www.thepsychologyofmission.com/

Introduction

I always knew that thoughts could become things. I just never knew how powerful thoughts could be.

Since launching my first book *Obstacles Equal Opportunities* in June 2017, life has changed significantly. My co-authors became bestselling authors and the second branch of my company was born. Follow It Thru publishing, and its growth led me to rebrand under my own name, Heather Andrews.

I saw for the first time with pure clarity what I was meant to do after I left my management role.

The path was paved, so to speak. Have there been twists, turns, ups and downs? Yes, but they have taught me lessons that I needed to move toward the growth we have experienced in the last six months.

Being an entrepreneur has made me stronger, love myself more, and more often than not, question my abilities and whether I have what it takes. It has tested whether I feel worthy of the life I want and deserve. It has made me question my true beliefs about what I am capable of and if one can really follow their passion.

It has taught me to get up and continue. It has shown me I am worthy of more, that I am capable of creating a seven-figure company and helping others create a life they desire and deserve. I am living proof that one can start over in the middle of their life with a dream and belief in your own self-worth. You just need to be open to lessons required for you to grow and know the power of connection and mentorship.

I have learned so much from my journey, and I wanted to share it with the world as I felt people would be able to relate. Once I put the project out to the world, thirteen beautiful women came forward to share their journeys of discovering their self-worth and self-love.

It is an ever-evolving process. Some may think that once you reset your self-worth gage, you are good for life, but life will toss you curves and it makes you question if you really have everything under control.

Please know that your belief in your own self-worth and self-love come from your inner beliefs and internal compass. Once I figured that out, the world became a different playing field.

I ensure that I always acknowledge my feelings and I have become increasingly aware of how things affect me. My co-authors have had the same experience.

Our wish for you is to embrace the stories, the lessons learned, and the mindset tips that are included from each co-author. Step into the knowledge that you are deserving of all things great and stellar.

It all stems from a thought that becomes a thing. When your thoughts change, it paves a new road for you.

Come along with us now.

Love,
Heather

What is Self-Love?
An Expert Opinion

That is often the question that gets asked because this mysterious word 'self-love' gets thrown around a lot, but no one truly knows what it means.

In fact, many people tend to see it as a negative concept, one related to narcissism. In fact, according to dictionary.com, the definition of self-love is the following:

The instinct by which one's actions are directed to the promotion of one's own welfare or well-being, especially an excessive regard for one's own advantage.

1. Conceit; Vanity.

2. Narcissism.

The concept of self-love is not always seen as favorable and positive. This definition reinforces people to continue shying away from giving permission to love themselves fully and completely, because it would seem vain, wrong and bad.

Let's go back to the true meaning of self-love.

Self-love is both a noun and a verb.

1. It is appreciating yourself like you appreciate a loved one

2. It involves engaging in thoughts and behaviors that align with this appreciation of yourself mentally, emotionally, physically and spiritually.

Scientist and author David R. Hamilton, in his book *I Love Me: The Science of Self-Love* describes self-love as "the essential regard for self that empowers you and helps you navigate through life. The type of love that enables you to feel safe and secure in who you are and inspires you to make choices that are good for your authentic self."

We are born into this world with loving energy. We just have to look at a baby and we immediately feel joy and love, cooing over its perfection. Then experiences and interactions people have with this baby will determine how this young being will eventually go into relationship with itself and others as he or she develops.

If that baby is born into a world of violence, and fear without its basic need being met, then the baby unconsciously forms negative thoughts and beliefs, he or she may feel shamed and rejected. If that baby is born into a loving, safe, nurturing world, and its basic needs are met he or she will form beliefs of feeling loved, wanted and belonging. These experiences stay with us on a cellular level.

At the very core of us, no matter who we are, we all have a biological drive to seek connections with others through a deep sense of love and belonging. Therefore, we often try to compromise parts of who we are authentically to win love and approval. However, this ultimately comes to a cost—our own self-worth.

We stop listening to ourselves, we tell ourselves lies to make things 'OK' when they really don't feel OK. We say yes when we really mean no. We lose our empowered voice to please others and to avoid the pain of rejection. We disconnect our head from our heart and soul, and we sacrifice our own self so that it creates a lose-win situation (lose for you, win for other).

All these behaviors show up because we are operating from a place of not feeling enough. We seek external validation, for someone else to approve of us. To validate the fact that we are worthy rather than us validating ourselves.

As women, we have a collective struggle around not being enough, not being worthy, not being lovable and not measuring up.

How does such a belief form?

When we are born into the world, we mostly live in our unconscious brain because the conscious, higher functioning, logical and executive functioning part of our brain is still developing in the early years. As infants, toddlers, and young children, we watch interactions between our family members and ourselves. From these observations, we unconsciously form beliefs around love, safety, belonging, trust, boundaries, power, money, sexuality, etc. We have no idea of how healthy or unhealthy that behavior is. We just think, *Oh this is the way the world works*. We insert ourselves in a way that allows us to understand who we are and how we survive in the world, so we can feel physically, mentally, and emotionally safe.

Often, even though it is not their intention to hurt us, our adult caregivers may project their own insecurities, anger, and embarrassment onto us. These acts can unknowingly and unintentionally create shame within us.

Shame is something that is put on us. It ultimately is about you believing at the core that something is wrong with you. Guilt, in contrast is about feeling bad about something you did. However, it is not about you being inherently flawed. Guilt is when a belief and a behavior are not in alignment.

From here, we learn to form core beliefs about ourselves and how we go into a relationship with ourselves and others. For example, if we operate from a belief of "I'm not enough," then we unconsciously create strategies to help us 'survive'. These strategies can be expressed in a variety of ways. One example from my own personal experience, as well as a common theme I see among my own clients, is that to overcompensate our belief of not being enough, we will become overachievers, perfectionists and develop a type-A personality.

In some ways, operating from this place can help us be 'successful', but because the root drive is coming from a place of lack, true self-love and fulfillment will not be experienced until the core belief changes from "I am not enough" to truly embracing and embodying "I am enough." When this happens on a cellular level, a new belief is formed.

Our beliefs are born out of survival; therefore, we wear them like a life jacket we created when we were young. As an adult, this same lifejacket will not really fit. We need to zoom out and look at life's bigger picture and see that the child within is still feeling vulnerable and trying to find emotional safety.

As a certified Hakomi practitioner and former registered psychologist, and now as a life and business coach, this is part of the foundational work I do with my clients. Once we embrace the truth of who we are, that we are enough as we are in our beingness, then we start to show up differently and most importantly, authentically—in alignment of who we truly are in the world.

When we truly love ourselves, we show up in our authenticity, which is the willingness to be vulnerable, the courage to be real and to be seen. Researcher and author of *The Power of Vulnerability*, Brene Brown, states that we associate vulnerability with shame, fear and anxiety and most of us do not like the edges of not knowing. Vulnerability leaves us open to pain and hurt. However, vulnerability is also the birthplace of love, joy, belonging, creativity and of course, authenticity.

So, what this looks like for myself and my clients in moving from a state of "not enough" to embodying and reclaiming "I am enough" is embracing being perfectly imperfect, living in the art of slowing down (without guilt), and showing up in vulnerability, even if fear of rejection and judgment are felt.

When we learn to love ourselves unconditionally we feel a deep sense of inner peace. When there is conflict between ourselves and other people, it is often because those people, often unconsciously, are mirroring us. They are shining back our darker parts—the parts of us that are undiscovered and unhealed. The more we work on self-love, the less bothered we will be by others' choices and actions because we will come from a place of love rather than judgment. This does not mean you have to agree with other people's choices and actions, it means you have more capacity to hold non-judgmental space for them because you hold space for yourself in the same way.

My wish for you is to know that you are a beautiful human being who deserves to live a wildly abundant life of self-love, joy and fulfillment. Keep evolving so you can shine your beautiful light and truth out into this world.

If you'd like to get in touch, you'll find my contact information in the bio before my chapter.

Rosalyn Fung

Heather Andrews

Lifestyle strategist, certified Follow It Thru health coach and international bestselling author, Heather Andrews initially created the inspiring Mom On The Go change mentorship program in a bold, immediate response to being 'restructured' out of her 'dream' management position in the beleaguered healthcare system. She was unaware of the extent of her resiliency or what this confidence-shattering experience would uncover.

Heather's veritable 'rediscovery' of her self-esteem, and her journey to the realization of a deeper, personal identity led her to ultimately embrace entrepreneurship wholeheartedly. With her own publishing company, and bestseller based on her signature story, *Obstacles Equal Opportunities*, as well as a foray into podcasting and internet radio, where she will host her own show, Follow It Thru to a Stellar Life. As a speaker, Heather inspires audiences by sharing her challenges and the survival strategies that continue to help her optimize adversity. Being a voice in self-discovery and revitalization, she is making a positive difference.

Find Heather online:
Websites: www.heatherandrews.press
                    www.followitthru.com
Facebook: www.facebook.com/followitthru

Chapter 1

Self-Love is Your Choice

By Heather Andrews

Why is it that in today's world we can talk about the bad things that happen to us and people comment on social media with empathy, embrace the negativity and root you on? Or better yet, agree and support you as you blame the situation or person for the bad day you are having?

Are you sitting there shaking your head in agreeance or thinking I am crazy?

I will agree with you on the crazy part, but it is a result of living a solid happy life on my terms. I support others in their dreams as they go out and create a different story for themselves. I refuse to live a life that is full of excuses and blame.

I have always been a self-confident career woman, but my sense of self-worth has climbed mountains and plummeted to the sea floor more times than I can count. I have played the empowered female, the victim, and the blame game. I have ventured down the road of being the biggest cheerleader at my pity parties to being in shock at someone giving me a compliment in my high-end managerial role on a job well done.

I was a people pleaser but viewed it as being a mentor to others. It did not matter what I sacrificed; whether it be family time, date nights, holidays, or self-care. Until recently, something or someone always came before me and my needs.

As I sat in my managerial office, I thought I had reached my full potential until I retired as I was highly esteemed, respected, and well known by my peers and industry.

I had it all. I was living the corporate dream. My identity was my titles: mother, wife and whatever else came my way, depending on what I was doing. The more I did, the more important I felt. I'm sure you'll be able to relate to that. It played havoc with my life without me realizing it because I refused to look and see where I was at in my constant 'doing'. I was stressed out, and it affected my relationships. I was not fully present for myself or for the people that loved me.

It looked all well and good, but even in my best moments in my job I second guessed myself that I was doing everything 'right' by other people's rules and expectations. I was trying to please everyone—to make everyone happy.

You can only carry a load like that for so long before you begin to crack, feel empty and start to resent everyone around you— including yourself.

I have told the story of me leaving my managerial role many times because it was such a life-changing event for me. It set the foundation for everything I have built with my mind, heart, and soul. I share my story again and again because I know people can relate to a job restructuring. People say, "It was just a job you will find another." True, but when your job is all you worked for—

when you are dying inside because you feel worthless, wondering how you will feed your family—that statement becomes nothing but bull crap.

It has taken me two and a half years to arrive at a place where I trust my intuition and can live a full, happy life.

I stand tall in my vision and my values, and I am proud of what I created. My social media feeds are some of the happiest out there because I have bottomed out and come back. I do whatever it takes because I am passionate, worthy, deserving and committed to my clients, co-authors, and even people I have not connected with yet. We are rising and changing the future for women, men and children for generations to come.

People tell me I am inspiring, and I am humbled. I am here to serve you by pouring my heart and soul into helping you share your story. I want to release people from their past and help them understand that they have a choice.

That word is powerful. CHOICE. It is the game changer! The day I got my walking papers from my job, even though I felt powerless, I knew I had a choice. When I left my dysfunctional marriage at twenty-four and got on a plane to Saudi Arabia, I had a choice. When my husband was deployed to Afghanistan, leaving me to solo parent three children, I hit my emotional wall and gained 30 lbs…I still had a choice.

When my dad died, and my mom was alone, I knew I had a choice. When I lost my job, I knew I had a choice.

The only time in my life when I did not choose well was when I chose to believe I was not worthy and good enough.

I chose to believe I was not pretty enough, not sexy enough, and not good enough because I was not skinny like a beautiful family member was who told me I was fat as a kid. It is amazing that I can remember that even though it happened so many years ago.

I have lived my life always wanting to be skinnier than I am. In the past, I based my worthiness on my waist size. It is crazy. Now, as I approach my forty-eighth birthday, I am the strongest, healthiest, and happiest I have ever been.

Why do we let ourselves believe we are not worthy? Why do we live in fear of what others will think, and how we will be judged if we fail? All this does is create internal conflict.

We live a conflicted life with what we hear, what we read, see, the upbringing we have had and the stories we tell ourselves and when we look in the mirror. We are conflicted with ourselves with what we see.

In a recent webinar, a mentor of mine said there were five types of conflict:

- Man vs. man

- Man vs. society

- Man vs. technology

- Man vs. self

- Man vs. nature

In this chapter, I will refer to man as human.

Human vs. Human

This one comes down to our interactions and connections with other people.

We have a choice on how we react to other people, the roles they play in our lives, and the impact they have in our lives. It goes back to what I said earlier about looking outside of ourselves for our self-worth versus looking inward and knowing in our hearts that we are unique individuals.

Once you recognize that you can either chose to believe what other people tell you or you can believe in your intuition and what's in your heart, what you receive in this world will change.

There is choice, but communication is key to translating what your choices are to those that are impacted.

When it comes to human vs. human, conflict occurs because people aren't always equipped to have difficult conversations with a win-win in mind. Words can hurt and cause harm if we allow them, especially if we are taking our cues from the external environment to measure our own self-worth.

I remember I attended a class in my leadership certification. The teacher mentioned that only 3% of society knew how to effectively handle conflict. Why is this not taught to our children outside the home? We would all be more empowered if we knew how to show up effectively by playing nice and really listening to what other people have to say. It's a lot easier to love yourself when you feel empowered.

Aha moment: I choose my words, so I am partly responsible for how they affect others.

Human vs. Society

Society is a tricky place. Social media is everywhere, and we must apply boundaries to our usage of it if we don't want it to consume us.

We are bombarded with photoshopped images telling us how we 'should' look. I remember thinking that if I looked like the women in these images, I would be happy. I know I was not alone in my beliefs.

In my first marriage, I believed that being in a subpar relationship was better than being alone, but I was alone anyway. We slept in the same bed at night, but we did not love or communicate with each other.

It also takes me back to when my husband deployed to Afghanistan, and my kids were in activities seven days a week. I was so fricking tired, and I had reached my max. I showed up to work in a bad mood—negative and full of blame. I made excuses for not eating healthy, I *deserved* my French fries. I was not holding myself accountable, and that is when I made a choice. I decided to cancel some activities and take back my life. It was one of the most empowering choices I ever made, and you know what, no one said a word to me. No one judged me and called me a failure as a parent.

Aha moment: No one cared because they were too busy dealing with their own chaos.

Human vs. Technology

Technology changes faster than we can keep up. It has connected us globally and having information at our fingertips is so powerful. We can build business teams online and communicate with friends near and far. We can see pictures of kids growing and talk face to face with our relatives in distant countries.

It keeps us close to what is happening in the world, and it can bring people together when they have a common goal.

The downside is we have become available twenty-four hours a day, seven days a week. Constantly being accessible and 'plugged in' can be very stressful and detrimental to self-love. Unless you turn off your device, you can always be found/contacted.

We like to be constantly busy because it makes us feel important and wanted. We often affiliate our self-worth to our little hand-held devices or computers. It is a symbol of self-gratification, if you want to call it that.

I am just as guilty of this at times, so now I have built boundaries around my devices and access them only when I need to, not because I *have* to. I made a choice to take control.

I have used technology to create automation in my life and business—so I can have a life.

Tony Robbins said, "Your cell phone is for *your* convenience, not others."

My son and I recently had a conversation about how technology was affecting his life. He is a third-year engineering student. He said engineering is still engineering, it is all the technology platforms that they had to learn that was an additional stressor to the amounts of content that they were being taught.

As I have raised my children, I have instilled in them the belief in themselves, and it has had its rewards, they have reached adulthood and met challenges head-on. He came home one day from university frustrated with the system. His words: "University is a great place for learning and connection, but the demands on you as a student can make you question your self-worth because it is so easy to feel like a failure. I can see why the suicide rate in my age range is increasing."

This came from his heart. He knows what he is talking about because he had a very dear friend commit suicide in his grade twelve year. I am not saying this to point fault at any institution,

I am merely stating an opinion, feeling, and observation from a kid in the system.

I knew I had my issues with my own self-worth, but it was not till I became a parent that I realized how much I needed to look deeper and to heal. I was their leader, mentor, and mother—the most influential part of their lives. If I did not have my beliefs intact and my internal compass of self-worth dialed up, what chance did they have?

In today's world technology has a global impact, so we need to be able to filter, set boundaries, only take cues from an external point of view, and hold on tight to your self-worth.

Aha moment: I had to be the one to choose to set boundaries regarding technology. I had to make a conscious decision to not affiliate my self-worth and love with how 'busy' I was.

Human vs. Nature

How does nature relate to self-worth or self-love? Well, we can view this from a couple of angles. Some of my best moments of reflection have happened in nature. For example, the gentle changing of one season to another. I can sometimes want things to change immediately, but nature reminds me that it is a gradual process.

Nature teaches us to weather the storm by overcoming obstacles that happen in our lives and it teaches us how to handle real-life situations. I talk more about overcoming them in my last book, *Obstacles Equal Opportunities*.

If one has been affected by weather, their lessons include recovery, patience, gratitude, overcoming loss, grief, resilience, and they gain the strength to move forward.

I am grateful for what nature has taught me and the places it has taken me—from the cold winters in Canada to the Saudi Arabian deserts.

The elements make you think ahead, and you need to be prepared with the right tools to keep you warm, dry, and protected.

If we walked through life being accountable for our preparedness, we might not take the hits we do to our self-esteem and self-doubt, which ultimately affects our self-worth.

Aha moment: Nature teaches us that while we have choices, we can't control *everything* in our lives. Sometimes we must go with the flow.

Human vs. Self

I wrote a post on my Facebook today about a course and its teachings that I have been practicing for eleven months. I attended one of the courses as volunteer team member.

Last year when I showed up at the course, I felt I had a pretty good handle on my life. I had my first book being published, and I was working full-time again. However, I was in debt because I felt I needed to upscale my business and ended up making some huge mistakes. I had tons of self-doubt, and my trust in myself and others suffered.

I felt I needed what other people were offering because I told myself daily I did not have what it took, even though my intuition told me otherwise.

I was very angry, but I deflected from talking about my feelings to talking about how busy I was because I did not want to look inward. I was scared about what I would find: pent-up old hurt, blame, excuses, and the possibility that I was not worthy.

A very brave man who I ended up being partnered with for the weekend had a strong sense of self, and during one of the exercises we had to look into each other's eyes. It was like looking into his soul, and I kept turning away because I was not sure I was ready for someone to see mine. It felt like a dark place—cold and unfeeling. He took my hand with purposeful kindness. No words were exchanged as he brought my eyes back to meet his.

The longer I stood there, the more I felt in my heart. Tears shone in my eyes. My tears came from a place of hurt, love, and kindness. They didn't come from anger over a job loss or feeling sorry for myself for what might have been, or the blame I put on myself for investing in my business or myself to the point of almost bankrupting my family. He stood there with kindness in his eyes, and nodded, as if he was giving me permission to feel again. That was the day I fought for what I believed, and told myself I was starting my business.

That weekend was the breakthrough I needed to bring my emotions to life and learn a new way to focus on the positive side of life. I had new tools, and my mind, soul, and body were working together in alignment.

This was my Facebook post from that day:

It all started with Flip Your Switch with Suze Casey eleven months ago. It amazes me how hard we are on ourselves. I attended the afternoon session today and gave testimony to my life transformed!

From the belief repatterning and way of being and showing up for myself and others in my life! I lead with heart!

I trust again and am so blessed!

By listening and taking a chance.

The results of my life are:

More loving human in my relationships.

Found my self-worth and trust within.

Have put a filter on the yucky stuff in the world and know how to move past it.

Empowered emotion.

Sense of calm, peace, and happiness.

Kicked fear to the curb.

Found my dream business which has grown 95 % in six months.

Trusted my path and surrendered to process.

Followed my gut.

Elevated my life.

We must lead by example. If I talked to anyone in my life the way I used to talk to myself at times, I would be friendless. I was mean to myself, and I allowed myself to believe that I was a worthless reject. There was no room for self-love among my self-hatred.

I did not respect myself enough to stop the negative self-talk, take care of my health, and trust in my inner guidance to know I could build my business without spending more money. The lack of trust also showed up as not completing any new course or sticking with any commitment.

My journey did not stop at that one weekend. I had many more universal slaps to learn lessons about self-love over the next four months.

I have utilized the tools I've learned on a daily basis to rediscover my self-love and self-worth. I have completed over one-hundred hours of transformational weekends and coaching. I have gone back to my childhood and dealt with every belief, statement, and negative piece of anger that I have carried. I have cried, written letters to myself, and beaten the floor with the angry stick, all in safe places with the guidance of professionals.

When I forgave myself for treating me so horribly I was able to grant myself permission to love me. I wanted to free myself from hatred and wrath and instead hold myself in loving arms. I allowed myself to surrender to the process. With the power of 'I am' affirmations and understanding who I was and what I stood for, I learned that I am a committed, passionate and deserving human who can love herself and serve others because Heather is an awesome human who cares so much for mankind and loves deeply.

Yes, I will grant myself the permission to say how hard I have worked to build my business, love those around me and hold them close. I have modeled the way and shown others that it is OK to love who you are and be that version of your unique self. I am proud of my Facebook post and what I have created in my business, my life, and my relationships.

I asked for help and support, and above all, I shut down the negative chatter. It has its time and place to keep me alive, but above that, I stop long enough to reset and ask my body, soul, and mind if we are all in alignment as we move forward.

I react, yes, but I do it from an empowered space, looking for resolve or lessons learned while holding myself accountable. Gone are the excuses, blame, and anger.

I know it has been working because for the last three months money has been tight, but we always had enough because I needed to spend time on my business producing and creating while working with my team on automation. I have found the resources to cut my debt in half, build my business by 95%, and finance the remainder of my loan.

I am happy and peaceful, and the more importantly, I love myself.

Since I have found my happy spot, my stress has decreased, my resentment and anger has diminished, and I have lost 22.5 inches from my body. We often come at our life's fulfillment with the concept of I will be happy when I achieve X or Y.

Well, what about happiness *during* the journey?

I know I have come at you from all angles in my story, but I wanted to share with you the real journey of what's self-love got to do with it.

My answer is everything. Your self-worth is your most priceless possession, it is your internal commodity and your value. If you are scared or stuck in your story, stop and look inward, not outward. What are you feeling right now? Acknowledge it by writing it down on the aha moments and self-reflections page after this chapter. In fact, I encourage you to do it after every chapter. We have provided space for you to do so.

What do you want to change? This is about you, your life, and your values. This is your story, and the choices you make will reflect the outcome.

Yes, it takes courage, support, and openness to break the barriers, but I know you can do it and I know you are worth it.

If you need permission, I give it to you with my heart and soul. Get on the worthy train and ride it until you find self-love. Dig deep and let it out. Share your story, it will help you heal, and it will help others to heal. The world needs our stories.

I know I have taken you on somewhat of a rollercoaster ride, but my goal was to share the many aspects to self-love and worth as it is more than a bubble bath and a glass of wine. Don't get me wrong, it's a great start, but that's what it is—a start. The journey is still ahead of you.

I stand strong today in my power. I am a parent, a woman, an influencer, a leader and mentor for our future generations. I am worthy, deserving, and owning my self-love.

My wish for you is to discover your path on the road of life. Take that first step today.

"You can't create different things if you are like everyone else."
-The Greatest Showman

Go be you and rock it like the rock star you are. Claim your self-worth, it is yours.

It won't always be easy, but once you make that first step, you won't look back.

Will you take that first step and cross the line?

It's your choice.

Lessons Learned and Mindset Tips

Lessons Learned:

1. No one can dream and create your dream but you. Others will share the journey, but it is yours for the taking.

2. Know without a doubt that you are worthy of all the great things in life and be open to receiving them. It is a game changer.

3. Fear is to keep you safe from danger but not keep you from following your dreams. Trust and surrender to the journey.

Mindset Tips:

1. Follow your inner guidance and intuition. If you can't hear it, stop and listen.

2. Your self-worth is an inside job, don't let external cues tell you what you already know. Your self-worth is the hottest commodity you have.

3. The best love affair is the one where you discover yourself.

Aha Moments and Self-Reflections

Note your Thoughts

_____

_____

_____

_____

_____

_____

_____

_____

_____

_____

_____

_____

_____

_____

_____

_____

_____

_____

_____

_____

Dr. Stacey Cooper

Chiropractic doctor, holistic health and wellness expert, lifestyle coach and author, Dr. Stacey Cooper initially created Lifestyle Balance Solutions in an immediate response to suffering her own health crisis due to a lack of balance in her life. She was unaware of the extent of her strength or what this life-altering experience would uncover for her and her family.

Stacey's 'rediscovery' of what it takes to be healthy in this crazy world, and her journey to the realization of a deeper relationship with herself and her family, led her to ultimately find the way to balance her life and restore her health.

Dr. Stacey has created online products as well as personal mentorship programs for her patients and clients. She has been featured in radio interviews with Gayle Carson and Darlene DeStefano, internet radio with Cheryl Ginnings and podcasts with Susan Cristallee. As a speaker, Stacey inspires audiences by sharing her story, her discoveries and the strategies that continue to help her optimize her health and wellbeing. Being an advocate for self-discovery, self-love, and revitalization, she is making a positive difference.

Find Dr. Stacey online:

www.DrStaceyCooper.com

https://www.facebook.com/DrStaceysNation/

support@lifestylebalancesolutions.com

Chapter 2

302 Days

By Dr. Stacey Cooper

Our little family had enjoyed a wonderful afternoon on that gorgeous day. Derek was just five months old, Kayla was two and Lyndsay was four. We had just moved into our new country home in May. The kids had settled early in bed that night. Life was extremely hectic, and my husband Dean, my high school sweetheart, and I just wanted to take a breather.

I just wanted my Calgon moment.

We had a new home, I had my chiropractic practice, and Dean was working shifts at the car manufacturing plant. We had a new hot tub, and we were going to take some much-needed time for ourselves. What happened next was beyond anything that I ever contemplated. It was my wake-up call.

We were enjoying the sunshine, the breeze, and the warmth of the water. This was our little piece of heaven. Then...everything changed in an instant.

As we were relaxing in the hot tub I started to feel heavy pressure in my chest, I was experiencing heart palpitations, I could not catch my breath. It was not long before total fear took over and I was completely panic-stricken. Without Dean by my side, I would not have made it out of the tub. As it turns out, I was in the early stages of a heart attack. Of course, that was the furthest thing from my mind as I was a healthy, vibrant, productive, thirty-three-year-old woman, with a young family, a new baby and so many people depending on me. There was no way this could be happening to me.

But it was.

We have been taught that we need to be Superwoman and that we have to do it all or we are considered weak. I am here to share with you a better way that I learned from this experience. This is why self-love is of the utmost and greatest importance and is my highest priority now because without self-love there is no health, vibrancy, love of life or existence for me.

I welcome you to join me on my journey.

Saturday, May 11th, 1996
Graduation Day

I graduated as a 4th generation doctor of chiropractic, from the same school as my dad and grandad. My great-grandfather started our practice in 1912 in our hometown of Brantford, Ontario. This was truly an incredible day for the entire family. Dean and I had been married for four years and he, along with both of our families, had supported me during my four years of university and for the grueling and intensive four years of chiropractic study. We were all very relieved, excited and emotional as my whole future opened up on that day.

Graduation was held at the University of Toronto, and we celebrated at the Royal York Hotel with our entire family. It was a day of pride, joy, accomplishment, and excitement and it truly touched my heart as my dad, and my father-in-law stood up and gave their speeches congratulating us. My dad was bursting with pride, and my father-in-law was thrilled to be able to welcome a doctor into the Latimer family. I was deeply touched when Dean stood up to share his congratulations and how proud he was of me and all that I had accomplished with all my hard work. He also then congratulated the new grandparents at the table. Yes, we were expecting our first baby! This was met with great whooping and hollering, tears of joy, lots of kisses around the table as well as the lighting of cigars, I might add.

Life continued to unfold very happily for us. Dean was working full-time, and I started practicing with my dad. Two months later Lyndsay was born, and two years later Kayla arrived. I was balancing my practice and my home life as I was in the office three days a week after an eight-week maternity leave with each of the girls. Being self-employed, if you're not in the office, you aren't getting paid, but the bills still come. My practice continued to grow, and Dad and I were working very well together.

Saturday, November 18th, 2000
Everything Changes

That was the day that everything changed, the day Dad was no longer able to practice.

Four years prior, Dad was diagnosed with chronic inflammatory demyelinating polyneuropathy. It is an auto-immune condition and had been managed, but on this day, he was no longer physically able to work. I was four months pregnant with our third child.

At that moment I had no concerns at all because of course I was *expected* to handle it all.

My life was turned completely upside down, and I do not ever remember a time when I felt such overwhelm. I had to interview and hire babysitters and then schedule care for the girls around Dean's shifts. The stress I experienced was incredible as I was managing the full caseload of two practices as well as running our business entirely on my own. We did not know if Dad would be able to come back to the office or not. There was always hope, but in the end, he never did return.

The month prior a very dear high school friend of ours had lost her husband due to an adverse medical reaction. She then found herself living in her childhood country home with her two young children all alone. At Christmas time she decided to move to the city, closer to her parents. She was thrilled to give us the opportunity to have a country property which we had always dreamed of. My dad's advice at this time was, "If this is where you want to be and what you want to do, don't let money stand in your way!" We were to become new homeowners.

February 2001
No Time for Relaxin

As much as I love practicing chiropractic, it was taking its toll on my body physically. Along with working full-time, we were also in the process of selling our home and packing up to move. I was very pregnant, and I was in the office adjusting patients forty hours per week. We practice full-spine manual adjusting, so my work is very physical. At this point, I had to wear a support belt to hold my pelvis and sacroiliac joints together. When the end of the pregnancy draws near, the body prepares by secreting the hormone relaxin. This enables ligaments to loosen and to allow the pelvis to open and become more flexible in preparation for the passage of the baby during delivery. I was working a lot. Too much. I was thoroughly enjoying each moment at the office, but as soon as I was in my car, on the drive home, it was all I could do at the end of the long days to crawl into an Epsom salt bath to relieve my aching, tired muscles, then straight to bed in order to just do it all over again the next day. I was missing my girls, my husband, and my dad. At that point, it was business as usual. There was no time to feel anything, the tasks at hand were too great to leave any room for feelings.

My due date was March 30th.

For my other two pregnancies, it was always Dad who took care of my patients while I was on my eight-week maternity leave. I did not have that option this time around, so I had to go through the process of hiring a locum who would be suitable to take care of our patients. We originally decided to have him enter the practice on March 15th, but we had him come into the office on Monday, March 5th instead. This turned out to be a very good idea.

Friday, March 9, 2001
Derek Arrives

Friday, March 9th started out just like so many other Fridays before where I would drop the girls at the sitters at 8 am. On this Friday Dean was working nights. He would pick the girls up at lunchtime, and they would all nap at home together. I was then expected to arrive home just after 4 pm. Dean would have supper ready, and then he would head off to work twenty minutes after I walked in the door. That was the game plan.

This is what actually happened:

I dropped Lyndsay and Kayla off at 8 am as planned. As I was leaning over two-year-old Kayla to unzip her coat, I felt a stitch.

This was three weeks prior to my due date, so I didn't think anything of it. On hindsight, that was the start of my labor.

I went to the office and continued to prepare the locum to take over our practice, and I continued to do the majority of the adjusting too. Occasionally, I would have to pause and stop to allow tension in my abdomen to pass. At noon I checked in with my midwife. She determined that what I called 'abdominal tension' was labor contractions which were one minute long! She then said, "You get yourself home, put your feet up and then we can determine whether this is false labor or not." Well, that was put on hold as Dad dropped into the office. He wanted to check on things and see how the locum was doing.

As I was giving Dad his adjustment, he asked how my day was going. That is when I said, "Well, I've been in labor all day." He just about freaked! He told me to alert Mom and to get myself home. I had not yet spoken with Dean. Boy was he going to get a surprise when I got home. I sorted everything with the locum, and I was able to leave the office at 3:10 pm. As I was barreling through Osborn's Corners shifting gears on the twelve-minute drive home, in my mind I said, *I dare any cop to pull me over now because they're going to be delivering this baby!* I was in transition!

As I arrived home and roared up the driveway, I cranked on the emergency brake, and I made it to the house hunched over and holding my belly. I arrived at the door and said to Dean, "Just tell them to come!" I knew without a doubt that this was not false labor, the baby was coming.

Dean delivered our baby boy on our bed with Lyndsay and Kayla rubbing my back. My mom and the midwives looked on from the doorway. Derek was born at 4:28 pm.

It was truly a magical day, and the entire family gathered that evening at our home for a birth day dinner to celebrate the first grandson. Everyone was so happy, and Dad said, "Finally, one with a handle!" There were already four granddaughters on my side of the family, and my father-in-law was so thrilled to have a boy to carry on the Latimer name.

This day was the official start of my maternity leave. Just two weeks later, my dad was admitted to the hospital in Hamilton.

Tuesday, March 20th, 2001
Dad is Admitted to Hospital

Dad ended up with cellulitis and was admitted to the hospital forty minutes away. Those days were filled with many obstacles and challenges. My mom and I were at the hospital with him to help when the nurses weren't available. It seemed like every single day there was more bad news. Dad was battling as hard as he could, but his body continued shutting down. It was heart-wrenching to see him bedridden when he had been such a strong, athletic, and active leader in our community. He was rapidly losing weight and having multiple adverse reactions to medications. It was grueling for all of us. His body was always one step ahead of what the doctors were doing, and not in a good way. He couldn't eat because of the sores in his mouth, he couldn't drink, he would pull out his pic lines...it was just unbelievable what he went through, not to mention the hallucinations and the mental anguish for my mom and him. At one point he said to me, "Well this sure is terrible timing." I had a baby in tow. The truth of it was that Derek was a huge blessing and enabled me to be with my dad during that difficult time. Otherwise, I would have been in the office full-time and at home with my girls and Dean, and I just wouldn't have had the time to get to Hamilton.

Saturday, April 14th, 2001
My Birthday

I don't even recall my birthday.

Winter was ending in Ontario and spring was dawning. My mom was looking forward to the day my dad would be coming home, and she had everything ready for him.

Derek was just five weeks old, and I was still on my maternity leave. I was able to spend a little more time with Lyndsay, Kayla, and Dean. Our house was sold, we just had to finish packing up our home and taking care of all the details so that we could move. I continued to spend time with Dad, and of course, I was sleep deprived because of our new baby.

Monday, May 14th, 2001
Our Dream Home

What an exciting day! The keys were handed over to us for our new home. The house was empty for the week, and all the contractors were able to get their work done before we were to move in on the Friday. With everything going on Dean and I were back and forth between the two houses all week, the girls were at the sitter's for part of each day, and I did not make it to Hamilton even once.

Friday, May 18th, 2001
Moving Day

The week certainly flew by. The movers delivered the girls' furniture, and all I had to do was make their beds. We decided to have their rooms painted identical to our previous home. It truly felt like home, and the transition was really easy for all of us. It was so nice to just get into bed that night and enjoy our new home in the country.

Saturday, May 19th, 2001
Dad was Stabilized

Dad called me from Hamilton at 6 am. Of course, if he was up, everybody should be up. He was so excited for us and the move that we'd made, and he wished that he could see our new home. We always valued the opinions of our parents and included them when we were purchasing our homes. They all had viewed the property with us in January when we were considering buying it. I told him that it would not be long before he would be over to see it. He was stabilized now, and we were just waiting for him to build up his strength before he was able to come home. What a day that would be. He had called me because he wanted me to come down and give him an adjustment. I headed down as soon as I finished nursing Derek. We had a great visit and stayed most of the morning. We then spent the rest of the day trying to start the process of getting settled at home, unpacking and catching up on a nap.

Sunday, May 20th, 2001
Laughter with Friends

Dad called Mom at 4:30 am to see if I could come back down again. He knew I was busy, but he had missed me over the last week (and I missed him too). All the time that he had spent in bed over the past nine weeks was hard on his body physically. I called him at 6 am and told him I would come down after lunch when the girls were napping. I had not seen the girls much that week either and family time was important. Mom came to the hospital a little bit later, and some friends visited too. It was a great afternoon with lots of laughs and memories shared. When Derek and I left at 4:15 pm I gave Dad a kiss goodbye and said, "I'll see you tomorrow."

5:17 pm
Finally Free

Derek and I had barely stepped in the door at home when the phone rang. The nurse asked if I could immediately return to Hamilton as Dad was not doing well.

It turned out my dad was already gone. He was 57. His body had shut down completely with a massive heart attack due to interactions with the medications. As I was racing back to Hamilton with Derek, I was always watching the highway to see if my mom was coming from the other direction so I could catch her on the way. When I arrived at the hospital and saw my dad all I could say was, "You are finally free." I was so happy that he was released from his suffering. I finally reached Mom at home, and all I could tell her was that she needed to come back to Hamilton. I could not tell her that Dad was already gone. She left immediately and refused to have someone drive her. I was able to have some close friends at the hospital for when she arrived, to help and support us. My younger brother was at work and was able to come right away, and our youngest brother was away for a long holiday weekend camping trip. Dean made the trip to bring our brother home.

One of the greatest difficulties was that my mom had never contemplated that Dad wasn't coming home. She had everything ready. The house, the yard, the pool, it was all ready for his return. She was completely and utterly devastated. It seemed like her world ended when her high school sweetheart left her.

While at the hospital I contacted a family friend who was a funeral director. I let him know that Dad had just passed, and I asked, "What is the next step?" I assumed that some arrangements had been made as Dad had been diagnosed four years prior, he had not practiced for six months and was hospitalized for nine weeks.

There were no arrangements made. We had to start at the beginning.

Every one of us has our own story, things left unsaid or undone. I cannot speak to the regrets that any of us may have had at the time of Dad's passing, all I know is that I felt like I had to support everyone during this time of huge loss because they were not just grieving, they were all suffering.

Next, we had to make the arrangements for my dad's funeral. Selecting a casket was quite the experience.

Thursday, May 24th, 2001
Dad's Funeral

The two days of visitation were a blur. I was still breastfeeding Derek while hundreds of people came to pay their respects. At Dad's funeral, I delivered his eulogy, with my voice wavering only once. I had not yet shed one tear for the loss of my dad. There was no time for that in my life. There was no time for me.

Monday, June 4th, 2001
Back to the Office

Life around me was carrying on 'as usual'. I was now supporting all our grieving patients who were missing their friend, their doctor, and their mentor. I had not yet allowed myself to grieve. I had to hire an associate for the practice as I could not do it all on my own. This added more stress and responsibility to my plate.

Saturday, August 25th, 2001, 7:30 pm
My Calgon Moment, NOT!

So here we are, the day of my health crisis when the events of the previous 302 days came crashing down on top of me.

I understand now that I was spared that day because my work here is not yet done and I was to bring our son Jake into this world too. That event is when I realized to my very core that my husband and our three children are my 'why'. I was determined to not let my babies grow up without me as their mother, and I would not leave Dean on his own.

You may already know that any stressor in life, whether it be a happy or sad event, will take your body out of homeostasis, the balance that the body attempts to maintain 24/7.

It seemed that I had all major life stressors, good and bad, occur within the span of 302 days:

- An enormous shift in job responsibility, Dad was no longer able to practice

- Huge uncertainty surrounding Dad's health

- The increased physical workload while being four months pregnant

- Purchasing our new home and applying for a second mortgage

- Selling our home

- Packing

- Derek arriving three weeks early

- Dad being admitted to the hospital two weeks later

- Received possession of our new home, moved in, and lost my dad all in six days

- Back to work one week later

- Having to support my mom, my brothers, my children, my husband, my patients, my staff, and everyone else *except myself*

Do you think that I was working just a little too hard? That my life was a little out of balance? Do you feel this way some days too? I was Superwoman. I could handle it all, yeah right! My body started to shut me down, and the time came that I had no choice but to listen. Sleeplessness, loss of appetite, dizziness, heart palpitations, missed beats, racing heart rate. This is what led to my health crisis. I was just thirty-three years old!

The big turning point was when my husband and our kids became my reason 'why', my reason to get balance back in our lives. It has taken some time, but we did it. We now have four beautiful children, I practice twenty-eight hours per week, and I have incorporated me time (this is a hard entry in my calendar) into my life.

What I do know is that our bodies are amazing at adapting to our environment. It handles change without you even thinking about it and informs you when things are out of balance. However, I have also learned firsthand that there is a finite limit to how it can adapt. I had no choice but to listen to my body because if I didn't, I wouldn't be here today. What I have learned is that I know that self-love has everything to do with it.

When grief and feelings are buried, the body loses its balance. The funny part is that your body does give warning signs, and they do start early, but we often ignore them because we choose to not deal with them. We tell ourselves, "it'll go away on its own". If I had done just that when I was thirty-three, then I would not have seen thirty-four, my husband would have been raising our three children on his own, and our youngest would never have been born.

It is much easier to correct a small problem than it is to turn around a major health issue, and for many, there is no second chance. As we know with heart attacks, they can come in an instant, and it can be over in seconds. I am one of the lucky ones.

Seventeen Years Later

Through these experiences, there are so many things that I have learned. It has taken years of study, trial and error, combining many techniques, protocols, and different teachings for me to be able to develop balance in my life, with self-love being the core concept of everything that I do.

I now begin every single day with me as the central focus because I have learned that if you don't take care of yourself, no one else is going to do it for you. Self-care is not selfish, it enables you to give more to all of those around you. Without your health and well-being, and when you don't take the time to nourish your mind, body and your spirit, you will suffer. You will live a life of exhaustion, you'll be over-worked, overwhelmed, frustrated, and living a life that you don't love. When you take care of yourself first, you then will be able to recharge your batteries, calm your mind to a peaceful place, and enable your body to be strong physically. This allows you to give so much more to all those around you, those who you want to serve, and this then leads to you living a life that you love.

I love pouring my heart into my clients to support them. I am here for you. For a complimentary consultation please contact me using the email in my bio above.

Lessons Learned and Mindset Tips

Lessons Learned:

1. Trying to be Superwoman is not attainable. It is unrealistic and creates so much undue stress in our already stressed out lives.

2. We should never feel like we must go it alone. There is no disgrace in asking for help. This is a sign of courage to realize and to ask for help when it is needed.

3. Self-care is not selfish. If we do not look after ourselves, no one else is going to do it for us. When we exhibit self-care, we recharge our batteries, reduce our stress, calm our mind and strengthen our bodies so that we may serve others to our greatest capacity. This then enables us to live a life we LOVE.

Mindset Tips:

1. Self-care is key so make YOU your priority. Are you even on your priority list?

2. Courage is to ask for help. It takes a community to flourish, and your community is there to help you. Take them up on their offer—you will be glad you did. I am so thankful for the help I have received from my friends and mentors.

3. Expand your learning. My baba lived to be ninety-three and always told me "So long as you learn something new, only then can you take the rest of the day off." Life is about lessons and expanding our knowledge. It keeps you young, vibrant and opens you to new ideas. Enjoy all that surrounds you and have FUN with it because life is too short.

Aha Moments and Self-Reflections

Note your Thoughts

_____

_____

_____

_____

_____

_____

_____

_____

_____

_____

_____

_____

_____

_____

_____

_____

_____

_____

_____

_____

Stefanie Davis-Miller

Stefanie is a mother, wife, paramedic and PTSD survivor. She advocates for people with PTSD/PTSI/OSI's to prevent them from suffering in silence. Stefanie shares her message through public speaking, offering a glimpse of her journey to help others struggling with mental health injuries and provide a voice for those who feel they are without. Stefanie is valiantly committed to her advocacy work surrounding mental health in the first responder community.

An Ontario Land Paramedic, Stefanie is currently the Wings of Change facilitator for the Brantford branch offering peer support meetings to the first responder/frontline worker communities where she currently serves.

Certified in M.A.N.E.R.S., A.S.I.S.T., and Road to Mental Readiness, (R2MR) training, Stefanie is the R2MR instructor for Brant County. She is an active participant in the development of a peer support program and currently sits on a committee with the county of Brant, developing a new C.I.S.M. wellness team.

Find Stefanie online:
Https://www.Stefanieespeaks.wixsite.com/17605
https://www.facebook.com/Stefanie.E.speaks/
https://www.instagram.com/stefanie_speaks/

Chapter 3

Growth Through Adversity

By Stefanie Davis-Miller

Perspective, everyone has their own. Their views are as their fingerprints, we all experience events in our own way. We perceive these events based on our lived experiences, culture, influences and age. Things as minimal as our day to day routines like purchasing your morning coffee, going for a run or driving to work, each time you do so is a new experience. Memories of the experience are recalled later and formed by your perception of what occurred. Recognizing this, one must be cautious to not judge another's interpretation of the event; just because you don't feel the experience was impactful, to another it could be pivotal.

As a paramedic, part of my assessment is to routinely ask my patients to rate their pain using a pain scale. "Sir, on a scale of one to ten, can you rate the intensity of your pain today?" It can be very difficult for some to come up with a number, if so I will press further and ask, "Can you tell me what the worst pain is that you've ever experienced, a broken bone? Childbirth?" This usually helps them by using qualifiers to base their answer. Many patients tell me they are in 10/10 pain while speaking in full sentences and present otherwise non-distressed. This 10/10 pain description can be describing anything ranging from a stubbed toe to someone who is severely ill or grievously injured. The same can be said for those patients who state they are not experiencing any pain or rate low on the scale, the injury or ailments can range from grievous bodily harm to a recent onset of the flu. The number is based on their perception of the pain.

Perception is based on personality, lived experience, culture, and social norms. Each impact the individual's reaction to experiences in a unique manner. People have often said that they don't know how I do it. My reply is always the same, "I didn't have a choice, I just did it." My answer comes from my perception at the time, we always have a choice. Thankfully, even in my darkest hour, my inner warrior was telling me to keep fighting. I can recall several times being told, "Wow, you should write a book." To that, I say...let's get started!

My inner warrior has always been present; although there was a period of time where she was barely audible, buried under a cascade of challenges that at the time were larger than life. Thankfully, she persevered, and through those struggles, I was molded into the woman I am today.

For ten years I have been extremely reluctant to share with anyone in the first responder circle the fact that I started my career as a paramedic with a previous mental health injury, PTSD. I entered this field with the perception that I was damaged goods. That any type of trauma response I would have would be directly linked to my previous experiences and diagnosis, in a sense making me a weak link in the first responder circle. First responders are tough, iron-clad and can handle *anything*. They are not affected by the repeated exposure to trauma, or are they? I felt because I was entering with PTSD, I had no place speaking out about this subject, and so although I have advocated for first responder mental health for the past ten years through volunteering, I have only recently disclosed my personal relationship. This thinking trap is *false*, this is a glimpse into what the injury can do to a person. PTSD shatters any form of self-confidence or self-assurance that you may have had. It crumbles you, consistently eating away at your very being. You trust no one, question everything and start to feel that there is *no good* in the world. You live in a constant sense of fear, question every ounce that kindness brings your way—and destroys it.

My college experience and subsequent hiring as a medic were extremely trying times for me, both emotionally and physically. My marriage was unhealthy and, at times, abusive. I was functioning for the most part as a single parent to my beautiful children, both under ten years of age at the time. I continue to carry my emotional baggage with me from years past, battling an injury that went unidentified for seven years. I was diagnosed with PTSD in 2000, by that time I had been exposed to several traumas. Any one of these exposures would have been severe enough to trigger an acute stress reaction. When left unattended, an acute stress reaction can merge into the diagnosis of PTSD, or as I prefer to call my personal diagnosis a post-traumatic stress *injury*.

In March 1993, my family and I were planning a trip to our condo in Florida. I didn't want to go but had no choice. I would have preferred staying at home with my friends; they were the most important thing to me at that time of my life.

The day before we left for Florida, my best friend Vicky had a few friends over to celebrate her birthday a little early and invited me to join. Instead, I made the boy I was dating my priority and only stopped in to see Vicky for about ten minutes before I headed home. I had planned to get her a gift while in Florida.

We arrived in Florida, and it was a little cooler than usual, we had to go and buy a couple of sweaters and pants to keep warm as we hadn't packed appropriately. There had been some severe weather warnings, but nothing out of the ordinary for Florida. On the night of March 12th, 1993, my family and I finished watching *Law & Order* around 11 pm and headed off to bed. It was raining hard. At approximately 3 am I was woken by the most horrifying noise, it was as if a herd of elephants was running across our roof. Terrified, I leaped out of bed to grab my younger sister who was in the other twin bed in the room to get her to safety. It took me several attempts to move her because she was frozen with fear and dead weight. I eventually got her up, and we ran into my parents' room and huddled together. The noise was the sound of our roof being ripped off the condo in what later I learned was called the 'Storm of the Century'.

Later that day I was finally able to get to a phone, I immediately called my friends to let them know I had survived. I didn't want them to be worried. I called Vicky's house, no answer. I called another friend's home and her little sister answered. The girl was in tears. She told me her sister wasn't home, that something bad had happened and I needed to call back to talk to her. I begged for the information, but she insisted I call back later. I hung up the phone thinking what could possibly have happened that was worse than what I had just experienced. When I called back a few hours later, my friend was still not home. I demanded that I be told what had happened and just like that it came, "Vicky's dead".

To say I was completely devastated would be an understatement. Growing up I moved schools approximately every two years. In grade eight my family moved from a small town where I attended private school to a new city and public school. I was alone, scared and in need of a friend to show me the way. Vicky and I had connected shortly after I started school and quickly became best friends. She was exactly what I needed, funny, outgoing, charismatic, fair, and someone I could trust and depend on. Going on five years of friendship and living in the same place with the same friends, this was the longest I had been able to keep a consistent friendship, Vicky meant the world to me. I flew home, alone. My mom offered to accompany me, but there was so much to deal with in Florida, and we had just arrived, I told her I would be OK, I was going to be with my friends.

From that day on my warrior, my protector, kicked into high gear. My strength was needed to protect everyone…everyone but me.

Two months later, the same friend mentioned earlier (the one I called and whose family delivered the fateful news about Vicky), and I were the victims of a brutal sexual assault. I was the first patient to receive treatment at the new sexual assault treatment center in my city. Not only did I have to come to terms with what happened, I felt like everyone knew. I had not yet processed the previous events, and now I was faced with another trauma. I felt like I failed and did not keep my friend safe. After the assault, the men who hurt us stated that we would have to stay put for a while, they were too intoxicated to drive us home. Thankfully, my parents insisted I learn to drive a standard shift vehicle. So, in that moment of desperation, my warrior took over and she drove their vehicle.

My warrior drove my friend to a safe location on the other side of the region. Doing so took me further away from my home, my safety, but I didn't care. My priority was to get her to a safe place. Once she was dropped off, I was alone in the vehicle with the men who hurt us. On the drive home, they remained in the back seat mocking me, making horrible comments. Regardless, I got myself home. The last thing they said was, "That was fun, we'll have to do it again sometime." I slammed the car door and sprinted to my house. Because of the assault, I was hospitalized and later referred to the sexual assault clinic for therapy.

At seventeen, I found that the therapy sessions did nothing for me. I agreed to go because I thought I had to. My expectation was they were going to fix me and take away all the pain I was feeling. That did not happen. What did help was the information. In school I was taking a law class, we had a year-end research presentation due. I chose to do my assignment on sexual assault. I was curious to learn about the laws, the issue of consent, and how and why charges were laid. I asked the clinic for some assistance and was given several videotapes to watch. On the tapes were many different women who had experienced a similar incident. What struck me the most was the, 'me too' element. There on the screen in front of me were women saying the same words, sentences and thoughts as I was experiencing. That presentation was a blessing in disguise as it forced me into action. It stirred something in me, the desire to learn and advocate for others, to grow through the adversity of the trauma. During my presentation, you could've heard a pin drop. I had the full attention of my classmates and my presentation went over the required time. I received applause from my classmates and an A+ from my teacher. This was my first experience with growth through adversity. This is also about as far as I got with my healing process.

Somehow, I made it through the following seven years even though they were filled with many challenges. Over the years I suffered, I didn't know I was sick. The numbness, hopelessness, emptiness, uncontrollable anger, risky behavior, suicidal ideations, and depression became my new normal. I've had some very dark times. I have held a knife in my hands, placed the blade on my wrist, and even taken pills. I understand this was due to my inability to cope. Action instigated by desperation, a cry for help. My injury crept in and took over my world. I had no idea that I was ill. By the time I was diagnosed I felt like it was too late. I didn't understand how bad I was or what the diagnosis of PTSD meant. I was thankful that someone recognized I had a problem and was willing to help me.

At the seven-year point, I had faced another couple of incidents, one of which caused me to crumble. The only thing that kept me from committing suicide was the fact I was pregnant with my first child. The warrior was still within me—the warrior who protects. There was no way I was going to do anything to cause my baby harm.

I was told I had PTSD, diagnosed by a psychiatrist and was placed on a regiment of pharmacotherapy and intensive psychotherapy that involved weekly evaluations with the doctor. As the months passed, I managed to continue to function. I felt I had no choice. I had a one-year-old daughter and a new baby on the way. My marriage was unhealthy and unsupportive, and it continued to impact the efficacy of my treatment plan.

As a result of an incident that happened at my workplace and the catalyst to my breakdown and subsequent diagnosis, I lost my employment. I was paid off with hush money to drop the lawsuit and I was not capable of returning to work. After a couple of years, my treatment was 'complete' and I had successfully weaned myself off the prescription medications. I don't remember my final visits, or the instructions given to me moving forward. Looking back, I wish I had been told that living with PTSD is a lifelong battle that requires constant work to stay healthy. With my limited knowledge, I assumed I was, 'cured', even though I continued to experience debilitating triggers, panic attacks, challenges with anger outbursts and suicidal ideations. That was my normal.

The safety in my home became increasingly more compromised, and I realized I had to do something. I began my exit plan with a career in paramedicine, which could support my kids and I financially and help others.

I began taking online courses to upgrade my studies, I joined the gym at the local college and began a rigorous workout plan. I knew this career demanded strength of character and body. I lost a couple of friendships because I was so dedicated. I couldn't attend coffee dates, I stopped drinking alcohol, I cleaned up my diet, and worked my butt off. I researched the program and went to meet the program coordinator before applying for the program to introduce myself and ask for any advice for admission. There was no room for failure, I was determined to be accepted to the college in my region. It was my only option, as I was also responsible for the kids. I secured a part-time job at a vet clinic to save some money and pay for my tuition. I applied in 2007, not expecting to be successful because I never felt good enough—a symptom of PTSD. I was one of thirty-two accepted out of over one thousand applicants into the paramedicine program.

I'm amazed I survived the two-year program. My first husband told me I wouldn't amount to anything. He threatened me and tried to sabotage everything I was doing.

I believe he was suffering from mental health issues related to his work in policing and earlier trauma. The issues got so bad at home that one of my instructors pulled me aside to ask if everything was OK. I told her I was fine. I suppose I wasn't masking it as well as I thought I did.

Throughout the paramedic program, I was on a rollercoaster of experiences. I was having panic attacks and had a car accident on the 401 with my son, which resulted in a back/neck/arm injury. I won a scholarship, and I made a lifelong friend, but the stress of completing scenarios would often drive me to becoming physically ill before it was my turn. Through it all, I persevered, never gave up and ended up graduating with honors. I was the recipient of the Mature Student Award. In 2017, I was recognized by Conestoga College with an Alumni of Distinction Award. In a way, I am glad I was told I was worthless, there's no stronger incentive to me then to tell me I can't do something. To those comments I received years ago I say, "Watch me go."

I have lived in the world of a first responder my entire life. My father is a thirty-two-year veteran of the Toronto Police Service, and my ex-husband continues to serve as a police officer. I recognize in them, as well as myself, some of the classic first responder personality trails that can be quite harmful:

- Being a control freak

- Being a king or queen of catastrophe

- Having a sick, twisted sense of humor

- Refusing to trust people

- Being bad at relationships

- Being a workaholic

I have heard stories told about police officers who just couldn't cope with the job. As the wife of a police officer I have experienced the emotions, struggles, personality changes and tolls this profession can cause. I remember desperately searching for some type of support group for other women like me, with no success. I felt like no one understood what I was going through. I decided along the way that something more needed to be done. There is very little support, recognition or acceptance surrounding mental health in the first responder community. There are no current statistics, but many of us come to the job having previously experienced an adverse traumatic event. A very common response to this type of exposure is to want to make a change, to advocate, to do better, to protect others from the experience of pain, and to help. You don't ever really, 'get over PTSD', but you can learn how to cope and move forward living a healthy, productive life. The danger for me and other first responders is the potential triggers I am exposed to while at work helping others. Currently, this is a very taboo topic, and although steps have been made to educate the first responder community about mental health and how our exposures can impact us, the fear of appearing weak, or unstable is still alive and well. The stigma is very much here. More needs to be done.

The number of first responder suicides is constantly climbing. This can be preventable. It wasn't until I learned of a former colleague's suicide that I decided to act and help the first responders I work alongside every day. I decided to share my own journey to help others. My philosophy is, if I can help just one person to understand that these feelings, behaviors, and personality changes are normal reactions to the exposure of traumatic events, then it is worth it. I want them to know that it is a human response and that it's OK to be human, that there is help out there. The scariest yet most empowering thing is when you discover that only you have the power to heal yourself and recover.

In 2017 I began the first responder peer support chapter in my community called Wings of Change, created by Natalie Harris. In October, I had the opportunity to share my story in two provinces reaching over six-hundred people. Since then I have been invited to several engagements to speak about my journey. In 2018, I was over the moon to speak at the Tema Conter Memorial Trust Education Symposium in Toronto. The Tema Trust is where I got my start with first responder mental health advocacy when I was awarded the Ontario scholarship for my essay in 2007. While in college, I submitted an essay on PTSD to a national competition. After becoming a successful candidate and learning about the Tema Trust, I made the decision to pay it forward, joined up to volunteer with them, and so began my journey in first responder mental health advocacy.

Accepting my PTSD as part of who I am is an ongoing battle. To say I no longer struggle would be false. I slip occasionally. When I'm in the shit, I tend to isolate myself from friends and family. Thankfully, through years of therapy, education, research, and communication my loving second husband lets me know when I'm slipping and is not afraid to gently suggest I seek help. I too am much more in tune with myself and can see things earlier than before and reach out. I have come to discover that it is not a bad thing to practice self-care and take a break when needed. It is not a weakness to ask for help, and best of all I now understand that I am not worthless damaged goods. In fact, through my lived experience, I have a personal wealth of knowledge that I can use to help others through sharing. I can be empathetic to those in need. I can relate to many different experiences. I also understand that when someone is hurting, it is not time to get on my soapbox and say, "I know how you feel." No one can possibly understand exactly how someone feels because that person comes to the incident with their own history. Through my experiences, I understand on a very profound level that when people are hurting what they need is to be seen, heard, and understood. I have also learned through my journey that education is a key to understanding and navigating through difficult times and exposure to trauma. There are many different, 'normal' reactions to such events.

My goal is to create a healthier first responder culture. I pay close attention to my moods and my reactions to them. I have an excellent therapist who continuously helps me navigate through my challenges. I understand that to stay healthy, I need to work on myself and be an active participant in my recovery. I know I'm worth the time and effort.

I am thankful for my experiences and the storms I have faced because they have made me a better person. Through my grief, sadness, and hurt something beautiful and selfless has evolved. It is amazing what you can learn when you allow yourself to be a little vulnerable, something that can be scary. My journey has been both terrifying and exhilarating.

It is possible to continue to live a healthy happy life after being diagnosed with PTSD. For me, it means I can continue to work as a paramedic, but it takes constant work, constant effort, and constant support. It is important to understand that while I can work in the first responder field and function effectively, I am an individual. It is not appropriate to compare my journey to anyone else's. We are all individuals. It has taken over twenty-five years of trial and error, to discover what works for me and what does not.

I believe my ongoing advocacy is part of my continued growth through adversity. I don't have all the answers...no one does. I am going to keep on trying and keep fighting with the hope that maybe I can help just one person. That perhaps through education and awareness, I can prevent just one from suffering this affliction. At the very least in normalizing these feelings, I hope to help promote understanding, support, and awareness. I am excited about sharing my journey moving forward through speaking engagements and completion of my book detailing my challenges and triumphs.

It's OK to be human. It's OK to love yourself, no matter what.

Lessons Learned and Mindset Tips

Lessons Learned:

1. The scariest yet most empowering thing is when you realize that you are the only one that can fix yourself. You must put in the work. No work, no result.

2. Don't listen to the nay-sayers…imagine where we would be if we all listened to them.

3. It's OK not to be OK. It's not weak to ask for help, it takes strength to do so.

Mindset Tips:

1. Life moves forward, not back, accept what you cannot change and move on.

2. Be thankful for each challenge you face, each adverse incident I have faced has taught me a lesson. These lessons make me who I am today.

3. People who are hurting need connection and support, don't be afraid to check in with your friend, family member or colleague if they don't seem quite right to you.

4. Be kind, you don't know the battles the person standing next to you might be facing.

Aha Moments and Self-Reflections

Note your Thoughts

_____

_____

_____

_____

_____

_____

_____

_____

_____

_____

_____

_____

_____

_____

_____

_____

_____

_____

_____

Adele Desjardins-Lepine

Adele Desjardins-Lepine has faced many adversities in her life. Some people look for escape in self-destruction or addiction...but not Adele. She has taken the lessons learned through pivotal points in her life to become co-dependent no more.

Adele is a child of divorce and a divorcee herself. She and her ex-husband have learned how to co-parent through communication and learning to lift the other partner even if they are not willing to reciprocate.

Today, Adele is a relationship coach, advocate for emotional survival and passionate about the well-being of others. She has learned that when you trust, that is where the magic happens.

She is dedicated to raising her two girls in Drumheller, Canada. She is full of gratitude, a pillar of her community, and a kick-ass friend!

Adele is excited to share the principles taught to her through positive psychology on how we strengthen our relationships, challenge our beliefs, understand love, and choose happiness so that we can succeed.

Find Adele online:
Website: www.adeledesjardins.com
Facebook: www.facebook.com/adele.lepine
Instagram: www.instagram.com/adeledspeaks

Chapter 4

From Co-Dependent to Happy Co-Parent

By Adele Desjardins-Lepine

I was raised by my dad in a single parent home. I learned at a very young age how to be responsible, take care of myself and, in some ways, raise my dad. I learned later in life that this is taking on a spousal role in a father-daughter relationship.

I felt that I never had a true childhood. I could not play freely, and I was not supported by my dad to just do kid things. Around seven or eight years of age, I became responsible for all the dusting, laundry, vacuuming and other household chores. My dad worked in the coal mine, and I was usually home alone, or he was napping before his night shift. Feeling abandoned at times, I began to wonder, *What do I have to do to be loved*? This is when my co-dependency began, and it stuck around for a long time.

I grew up feeling ashamed of my feelings, my wants, and my needs. I was told how I felt and was judged when expressing my true emotions. My dad regularly questioned my actions. This felt like a judgment of my existence—that it could have been done differently or better somehow. As a coping mechanism, I tried to predict the outcome of a situation and please my dad. For example, I was really good at making sure my chores were done, or I would do extra cleaning in the bathroom or organize cupboards. That way, my dad couldn't say no when I asked to go play. I would have conversations in my head over and over to predict a situation.

This was how I learned to solve problems. My dad liked to party and made his schedule his priority, so I walked on eggshells, making sure to never upset him. I made it my life's mission to take care of him if he had been drinking. I became hypervigilant, observing how many drinks he had and if he had eaten. I even took responsibility for his friends and worried about whether they too would get home to their families for supper.

At the age of fourteen, I had my first real relationship. I dated a man that was five years older than me. The age difference didn't seem to matter as I was mature, and thankfully he was not interested in an intimate relationship at the time. I dated him only because my best friend was dating his best friend. There wasn't attraction on my end, but he took care of me and seemed mature and stable.

My dad always told me, "Marry for money, love will come later." I guess I was waiting for love. This relationship lasted through my high school years, but it didn't fuel my soul. In fact, I felt anger and resentment that I accommodated him to avoid a breakup. Eventually, I could finally use college as an excuse to end the relationship. I was relieved, even though my dad judged me. He was very upset that I was "throwing away" four and a half years. I felt controlled in the relationship and didn't have the freedom to do the things that I wanted. Still, I felt a void when the relationship ended. Who was I going to take care of? Who was I going to fix?

Two weeks after the breakup, I was in a new relationship. I met an amazing-looking guy living in my apartment building whose roommate was dating my roommate. We had fun times together, and he showed me that sometimes life can give you hurdles, but all you need to do is jump over them, keep going, and have fun. It made me realize that my life really wasn't that bad.

He was unemployed and loved to spend most of his time at the gym. I didn't think these were red flags. I had someone to take care of again. Within weeks I told him that I loved him. I think I was on a high due to all the change and excitement in my life. It took him a few more weeks to tell me he loved me too and within six months I proposed to him. He said, "Of course." I assumed this was what love looked like. Why would I want anything different? I could replicate the relationship modeled to me in my childhood.

Our love was dysfunctional. There were emotions of despair, hopelessness, and shame. He had such low self-esteem that I figured it was my duty to lift him up and make him feel whole as a human being. In doing so, I did not know my own needs and my own feelings.

After my first year of college, I decided not to finish my program. Often, I worked two or three jobs to support us as he struggled to find employment or anything that he enjoyed doing. He had gone to school for corrections, but he didn't feel that he would be successful in the field so struggled to put in the effort to apply for jobs. I took it upon myself to find the mailing addresses of institutions to send his applications.

After nine months he was offered a position with Corrections Canada. It meant moving away to the town of Drumheller, Alberta. I would have to give up a career that I loved, working with disabled adults, and move to a community I knew nothing about. But I went with it. I found us a place to live and set up our new home so he could focus on training. I struggled to find employment and make friends. He told me that once he was settled into his career, I could go back to school or do whatever I wanted. This gave me hope.

Unfortunately, he never seemed to enjoy his job and was always searching for something better. I often found myself deeply involved in helping him, from doing up his résumés, to job searches. I invested so much of me into his troubles.

At this point, he decided to do a bodybuilding competition. That meant more work for me, and I became even lower on my own priority list. I prepared all his meals, making sure his complicated diet was labeled, so he didn't even need to question what container he was supposed to eat first. I was responsible for counting all his calories and making sure that everything was correct in his diet plan.

He repeatedly blamed me for any poor outcomes or miscalculations. I felt judged in the same way that I had grown up with. He forced me back into my co-dependent ways. I made sure I predicted the outcome of a situation by holding conversations over and over in my head.

As the years passed, he struggled deeply with his own self-esteem and acceptance. He coped by turning to alcohol. This was something else I was used to. I remember pleading with him to please forgive me—as if I were the only one who made mistakes. I was a co-dependent. I was not able to communicate what I felt or express my needs and my wants. Instead, I had hidden expectations, I would manipulate, hint or even become passive aggressive. This is not who I wanted to be, and I needed to change it, but I wasn't ready yet.

After five years of marriage, and much convincing from me, he agreed to start a family. After having our daughter, I felt like I had a purpose, but that didn't solve any problems. We didn't have the same parenting styles. In my mind, I knew what was best for her, and I was going to be the mom that I never had. Yet, I was constantly questioned and judged on my choices and care.

Over the next few years, we moved three times, leaving and returning to Drumheller several times. We left beautiful homes and good friends to chase a new job and a chance for happiness. Inevitably, none of the moves worked out, and within months the depression and drinking became a solution. So we moved again. This cycle continued because I did not feel my jobs or desires were important. I left and gave up my jobs to try to make him happy. To take care of his needs. Though I realize it was irrational, I picked up and moved back and forth to avoid fights, to pursue the one chance to fill his voids. Of course, none of this worked.

His mental health became the forefront of my existence. He had such strong needs and desires that many times I would do things that didn't align with my values because I didn't know any other way.

Two children, twelve years of marriage and three moves later, I began counseling. I was starting to journal my thoughts and my feelings. I knew my enabling was wrong, but I didn't know any other way. I felt shame for allowing someone to control my life all those years. I had low self-esteem and didn't think that I was worth anything more. We attract the love that we think we deserve. That was definitely true.

The final move back to Drumheller did nothing for our marriage. The drinking continued, and he was in such a deep, dark space. I still felt that it was my job to stand beside him as he struggled through his depression. I was strong and resilient, and he needed that.

Due to the financial losses from moving so often, we could only afford a tiny home. However, once our financial situation improved, I gave him an ultimatum. We were either going to buy a larger home and work on our marriage, or he could stay in this little house, and I would leave. He chose to find a larger home and work on our family.

Yet again, as he was so good at it, he gave me hope. Yet again, I believed it. We moved into the new home and rented out our little house, which provided extra income. We entered counseling to see if we could come together and figure out how to communicate in a functional way. Things seemed to be getting better, and there would be bouts of sobriety and bouts of hope.

But four months later, he told me that he no longer wanted to do this and was leaving the marriage. I was completely shocked. I once again became his rescuer and found him a place to live. He was so out of touch with reality, he didn't realize that he chose to move out on Mother's Day. I thought, *How could he pick a day that means so much to me, that's about me being the mother of his children?*

Telling our children was the hardest thing I had to do. I felt that all my years of hard work on our marriage had failed. For years I held onto hope—and for what? He lived in an apartment above my workplace for four months.

That September he moved back into the family home. We were going to work on things. This time around was no different than the past thirteen years. I would have moments of hope and then disappointment. More hope and more disappointment. I continued to enable behaviors, find excuses, and do anything to save my marriage. My dad pleaded with my husband to put my family back together. My dad had not been well, diagnosed with lupus years previously. I believe my husband came back home to try to please my dad. After only two months of getting back together, my dad passed away. I wondered how long I could continue living this way: the hurt, the lack of respect, and the many, many nights of crying myself to sleep. Could I continue to protect my children from the effects of alcohol and a dysfunctional family?

My journal at the time contains entries like, 'I feel alone', 'I miss feeling loved', and 'I am sorry, please forgive me'. Why was I asking for forgiveness, almost pleading at times? My behavior was so sick.

One entry dated in 2011 said: 'I have sacrificed so much in my life just waiting for my turn, for life to allow me to take care of myself first. It has been so long I don't know how to anymore. I feel lost and out of control. I am always concerned about making the people around me happy. I can't even make my husband happy. I have failed at my life's achievement. Is it me, what's wrong...how can I FIX IT?'

I finally asked in the journal, 'How do I become a stronger ME?'

January 2014 is when my life turned around. I discovered self-worth and that the first person you need to love is yourself. I attended a conference to invest in my own personal growth and discover what it was I wanted in life. One exercise I participated in was envisioning my life a year later having made the changes and accomplishing the goals that I set that weekend. As I did this assignment my first words were, "I am alone." I saw no one sleeping in my bed; I saw only my clothes in my closet. I had money in my bank account as I only needed to take care of myself and my girls. I saw that I was happy. I realized I didn't need to fix anybody but myself.

I felt so many emotions that weekend. I remember being paralyzed when asked to write a list of one-hundred things I wanted to accomplish in the next ten years. I couldn't even start. I didn't know how to want anything for myself. The first thing I wrote was, 'Move to Australia'. I look back now and see that moving wasn't ever my dream. It was his. I was only able to get to forty things, and only a handful of them were about me and my wants. With more sessions and hearing more speakers, I recognized my fears and triggers.

By the end of the weekend, I had changed my language to, "I am worth it, I am beautiful, and I am FREE." I had the strength I needed and knew that my marriage was over. I was tired of the moments of hope that only lead to despair, crying myself to sleep and disappointment. I had also recently learned that hope can carry a co-dependent six months before they had enough. This is what got me through sixteen years of marriage. I was ready to fight for me.

To do this, I had to ask myself some hard questions. The first being what was my 'why' for being married. The best answer I could come up with was, "So I am not another statistic of a failed marriage." When I said that out loud, I realized that was the dumbest possible reason for being married. I questioned what others would really think if my marriage had failed. Would they care? I imagined what my gravestone would say. It wouldn't say, 'She lived fifty years of a dreadful marriage, but, hey, she did it!' Nor would it say, 'She was divorced at thirty-five and a b***h.'

What I did know is that my children would question why I didn't leave sooner. I had repeatedly heard other children of adults in late divorce ask this of their parents. I also took this time to consider my family members that were either still in their marriage or had been divorced. Some have been married repeatedly, others never married again, and some are still in a long-term marriage. I concluded that none of it mattered; no one in my family was judging them. I wasn't going to be another statistic, but what I was going to be, was happy.

One night I told my husband I was done. I knew in loving myself and him it was time to let go of the dream that our marriage was going to flourish. I knew that the apartment above my workplace was available again as I had spoken to my boss the week prior. I told her I needed the keys to the apartment and went up to check it out, even though I was quite familiar with it.

There was something new on the wall. It said, 'Dance like nobody's watching'. I had written those exact words in my new journal and on my vision board that I had built at my transformation weekend that January. I knew at that moment this was exactly where I was supposed to be and the journey that I was supposed to be on. I went home and told my girls that we were moving out, that things were not well between their father and me and that I needed to do this for me. I felt so selfish, but the pain was so great, and I was done being the enabler. I gathered boxes and filled them with my stuff while he sat and watched. In two days, the girls and I were moved into the apartment with all our boxes unpacked. We quickly settled into our new existence. I finally felt free to be myself and to be the mom that I always wanted to be for my girls.

I believe divorce was a good thing for me. I learned to give without expectations, how to relax and what was self-care. I also learned that I wasn't a failure. I was learning from the things that I failed at instead of repeating the behavior. This was all new, so I was open to advice. I talked freely with others to gain knowledge and was open to change.

It had been eighteen years since I lived on my own and made all my own decisions. It felt amazing! I was finally able to use my voice to express my needs and to say no to my ex-husband without guilt. I no longer had to take care of him. It wasn't my responsibility to create his happiness. We were communicating better than we ever had, always putting the needs of the children first. In doing so, I had to let go of some issues that really didn't matter at the end of the day. I set boundaries and if they weren't being crossed, was I willing to change my ideals or beliefs? Many times it was a yes, as long as my girls were happy and it didn't sacrifice my great co-parenting relationship with their dad. This has led me to a new career as a divorce and co-parenting coach. I teach clients that we can come out of divorce solvent, happy and enjoying life. I believe if we are financially sound, then we are happy, and if we are happy, then we are enjoying life. A good rule to remember is that approach determines response. How you approach a conversation will usually determine the response you get.

There is so much negative talk about divorce, and I want to change that. My divorce journey has been great! My ex-husband is not an asshole, and I am not a gold digger. Together we are learning and supporting each other to be great parents. We are still a family unit; we just don't live together. Also, the children didn't ask for this life, so they shouldn't have to suffer. We can attend school activities, go for suppers and celebrate birthdays together with laughter. My girls never need to choose which parent they can be with. This didn't happen overnight. Together we have worked on open communication, we attended family counseling and learned to be able to share our feelings without judgment. Every day I am reminded why I chose divorce. I did it because I love myself. It has allowed me to teach my girls they have a voice, they are entitled to an opinion, and they are valuable. Speak up, you will make a difference. Don't be a doormat.

With my divorce comes gratitude. I have learned that we all have choices and sometimes those choices are harder than others, but with them, I have built strength and resiliency. I am thankful for my childhood and for my marriage, as they have taught me how to be a lover, not a fighter. Being a co-dependent and unaware that there were other ways of communicating in a healthy fashion cost me a lot of years of not doing what I wanted to or knowing what it was that I wanted.

I now know that I am worthy of self-love and the love of others. I am no longer co-dependent. I sometimes have triggers, but I can talk through them, and I no longer enable behaviors. I am constantly evolving and learning new techniques, attending seminars on self-growth and always staying open to the possibility that there is another way. My greatest strength comes from the realization that I do not control how others choose to react to what I say or do, but how I choose to react is entirely within my power.

Lessons Learned and Mindset Tips

Lessons Learned:

1. Life is about choices. We choose our mindset, we choose our beliefs and how we interact with others. You have the power to change your choices.

2. I can detach with love. I won't always agree with others, but I can set boundaries, express myself freely and give them space to be themselves.

3. Don't be a doormat. Use your voice and free yourself from being a co-dependant.

Mindset Tips:

1. Persevere. Desire to learn and desire to grow.

2. FAIL stands for First Attempt in Learning.

3. If I don't take responsibility, I can't fix it.

Aha Moments and Self-Reflections

Note your Thoughts

Alana Dixon-McAllister

Alana is an author, life coach, herbalist and wellness advocate. Her passion lies with helping others achieve their dreams of a healthy lifestyle and mindset. She is big on making her community a safe space for adults and children to be able to express themselves with no limitations.

Overcoming her battle with health issues like her lupus, depression, failed relationships, divorces and mental instability, she was able to move forward and find the self-love she deserved to grow in ways unimaginable. Life was not able to hold her back, but it slung her forward to a whole new level.

Alana believes that by sharing her story she will be able to give the courage to the next woman who may be struggling with where she is sexually in her life. Building those up in need of just aiding as a stepping-stone to find a self-love routine that works for them.

Find Alana online:
www.facebook.com/DelightsByAlana
www.facebook.com/CoachLanaMac
www.EmpowermentOfTheSoul.com

Chapter 5

I Killed My Vagina

By Alana Dixon-McAllister

I'd never heard the term self-love until a few years ago. So, what is self-love? How does one achieve such love when love has never really been shown? My definitions of self-love include: being vulnerable, saying no, masturbation, self-exploration, sensuality, calmness, finding inner peace, massages, saying yes to self, taking care of yourself before anyone else, trust and so much more.

All my life I have been Alana, 'The Mother'. Not as a mother in the giving birth kind of way but mother as in caretaker of others. They called me and still do call me 'Mama Lana'. I was/am the one they called when they needed advice, help or comfort. The Leo in me took pride in that joy of being wanted. Even if it was in a negative way like domestic violence and verbal abuse. I didn't enjoy that part, but this was something I felt I could fix. This was my destroyer. This sunk my battleship.

I thought it was my job to fix my exes. It took me three back-to-back relationships to see this was not for me and I needed a way out. A change. I know now that what I needed was self-love.

The abuse took its toll on me. I didn't know who I was, what I wanted or how to live my life. I was in constant fear, and everyone still came to me requesting my help. Yet no one could see I needed their help. My strong demeanor, exterior facade made everyone, and sometimes myself feel as if I had everything under control. I was depressed; I was broken; I was lost. There were a handful of times I almost had myself committed to the psychiatric ward. I was prescribed depression meds, and I thought I was losing my mind. I would sit in the car and cry. I would go to work and cry. I would go home and cry. No one, not even my family saw my tears. I had to be strong for everyone else, but I couldn't even be strong for myself.

The abuse I endured for years broke me down so far that I lost all hope. I had so little trust in others that I built a wall. The bruises on my body, the black eyes, and the canceled plans were clear to see. Yet still, no one asked, "Are you ok?" or, "Do you need me?" or, "Let's go talk about how you are feeling." Absolutely nothing. Looking back at it now, it wasn't them, it was me. I put up the impenetrable barrier because I was embarrassed. I was afraid of what people may say about me. I didn't speak up and let those closest to me see me in my most vulnerable state...Broken. I isolated myself. Just so no one could find me. To them, they just assumed I wanted to be alone and not be bothered. Which is true, but I wanted them to fight for me, and they did. I just didn't accept it.

I felt like I was sinking without a lifeline. I became a zombie to life. Moving from day to day going through the motions, slow motions. Throughout all this turmoil, I lost my sex drive. Say what now? Yes, lost it. Poof, it was gone. Let's say that level 5 was normal. Well, my sex drive was at level 0 compared to a level 20. I was used to having sex when and how I wanted. I used to joke around that my vagina was broken. Trying to make it not so serious. Being in my twenties, that wasn't supposed to happen. It's funny now, but my vagina died when I lost my spark. Sex wasn't pleasurable anymore. It became more about trying to make a child with the wrong men than just having sex at all.

After my abortion at the age of twenty-one, I thought if I had a child I would be able to make up for what I did. I wouldn't feel guilty anymore. I felt like I would be able to forgive myself for my actions and things would be back to normal. Luckily, I didn't get pregnant by any of them. Sex was all about procreation, it felt like work, and I was so not into it. I was stuck using different lubes that caused major issues with my vagina. It caused more dryness. It caused infections and swelling. My poor vagina felt like it was something that people kept recycling but never restored it back to its original settings. #DeadButNotForgotten

I had to stop having sex. It was too painful and too depressing. I even tried using vibrators, and it was like how I feel about black coffee. Just bland, blah and what's the point if you can't add some flavor to it to spice it up. Just throw the whole cup away! Ironically, I could see myself as Samantha from Sex in the City in the episode where she overused vibrators and couldn't feel anything anymore. That was me. That was my real-life story. I felt her pain, and I just wanted to see her have pleasure again. Poor Samantha. Hell, poor me! Life is supposed to have the feels, the tingles, the caresses, the body quivers and here I was with a dead vagina. "I want my tingles back!" That was me crying, not over spilled milk but my vagina.

This lasted a few months. It wasn't until I reunited with a friend from high school. This dude was younger than I was by about three years. In high school, I was not attracted to him at all. He was so tiny and young. All I ever dealt with were men much older than I was. But seeing him now or I should say then, made my floor hit the jaw. I mean, made my jaw hit the floor. He was so damn handsome, he used to make me mess up my words. Unreal. We started to become reacquainted with each other. I remember like it was yesterday, he made me feel so comfortable in his presence, and he listened to me vent. He gave me his full attention with no questions asked. The way he gazed into my eyes listening to me intently shifted something inside of me. During one of our chats, he softly grabbed my face and kissed me. I almost fainted. I turned into putty in his hands. It was so passionate and deep it unlocked the tingles I missed so dearly. I wasn't ready then to give him what I wanted for fear that what I felt was just a hoax. I didn't want to turn him into what I had done with the others. So we kept things at bay. Don't get me wrong I did eventually have sex with him; that was inevitable. But I had to make sure that what I felt was real. My vagina wasn't broken, it was just asleep waiting to be awoken by a real prince. But it was definitely under a spell.

After he and I parted ways, I moved to a new city. This is where my transformation really came into play. My vagina and I were on better terms, but self-pleasure was non-existent. My vagina went back under the dormant spell, and if any man looked at me, she would frown up and say eewww. "Death to men," she chanted. No one was good enough for this viewing pleasure. I did end up meeting my now husband through a mutual friend eventually, but we were in a long-distance relationship. My life was starting to feel normal again, adjusting to new living situations and WHAM! I became ill.

I was alone, sick and confused as to what was going on. I started breaking out in hives all over my body. I had many doctors' appointments, lots of pills and creams but nothing helped it. I started researching online about hives and came across an article that spoke about black women, their hair and health issues. It was like I was reading about me. All my life I had a perm. Not a curly perm that most know about, a straightening perm for kinky hair. It's linked to black women having ovarian cysts like I had; it's linked to hives like I had. It's linked to infertility like I had. It's linked to hormonal imbalances and to so many things that I said, "Enough is enough!" My inner-self said, *It's time to make drastic changes, and today we are starting with your hair.* So, I listened, I found a beauty parlor and had the beautician shave my head bald. Now that was an experience in itself.

I sat in the salon with my heart pounding. The beautician asked if I was sure and I responded, "Please do it right now before I get up and chicken out." She said, "I normally don't just shave people's heads without a consult, but I feel you're ready. Plus, you have a nice shaped head. If you had a messed up noggin, I would have told you no." We laughed. She took my ponytail out (my hair was shoulder length at the time), grabbed a handful of hair and cut it. With each cut section, she would stop and look at me. I would just nod like, it's OK just keep going. This moment made everyone in the salon stop. The other beauticians and their clients walked over to me and just stood in amazement. As my hair was being buzzed off with clippers, I was asked what made me want to do this, and they told me how brave I was. This moment was the beginning of my everything. The start to self-love I hadn't even discovered I needed yet. The beautician finished up and handed me a mirror. I looked at my reflection and wanted to cry. I had never seen my face before. Well, at least not like that. I didn't know how I felt about it, but I was free. I went home that night and posted my 'New Me' picture on Facebook and people went nuts—in a good way. People were saying, "I wished I could just go shave my head and not feel weird about it, you look amazing." That night I went to bed and laid my head down. That was the most interesting feeling, not having a barrier of hair blocking the energetic connection between my pillow and me. It was cold, but it was bliss. The next morning I hopped in the shower and got my hair wet. At that moment, I knew I made the right choice—I didn't even have to do my hair! Just get up and go. It was the best. It was the beginning to what I called, The Berkley Effect. Basically, those from Berkley area are all about the organic lifestyle and movement. That's what I modeled how I wanted to live on.

Next on my list was revamping my lifestyle. Food and body care products. Now that I was starting from scratch and rebooting my system, I was in the right headspace to try everything new. Nothing scared me anymore. I went vegan, I learned how to create my own body care products from scratch and life started turning around. My rash went away, and I was ecstatic. No more itching! It was all because I changed up a few habits and worked on clearing and cleansing me. Six years later, I still make all my own body products. The more I learned about natural ways, the more I began to discover me. It was like a new door opened up. My friends online were changing. I started meeting herbalist, vegans, crystal healers, reiki masters and more. They showed me a world I had no clue existed. They also showed me how my new-found journey could turn into a business. It was magical. While talking to the herbalists and healers, I came across a woman by the name of Queen Afua. She's like the mother of all women in this world. Her teachings on women's bodies, health, sex, and religion and spiritual guidance give you the tools you need to find yourself. She helps you dig deeper into the spirit realm and shows you how living for you should really be. Queen Afua takes women on a spiritual healing journey from trauma to self-discovery to seeing your wombman hood (yes womb, as in the birthplace of all life), to be the queen you are. Respecting your body by monitoring who you allow in your space, the foods you consume, the thoughts you have and life you live. This is when I found out that self-love was real.

All life forms begin in the yoni. Yoni is Sanskrit for womb (aka sacred place). We hold negative energy, trauma, past relationship and sexual partners in this space. When we get angry, the emotional turmoil resides there. You have to learn how to release it and clear it to activate your chakras so you can heal.

When we come up with ideas, this is where we birth them. Your womb is located in the same place as your sacral chakra. There is a total of seven chakras within us, more around us but we mainly focus on the seven. The entire universe is made of energy, and your body is no exception. Long before modern technology and science, ancient cultures knew that all living things carried a life force with them. They called the centers of energy that move inside of us, the seven chakras. Starting at the base of the spine we have the root, going up to the sacral, then the solar plexus, up to the heart, and then the throat, to the third eye, and all the way up to the crown just above your head. In a healthy, balanced person, the seven chakras provide exactly the right amount of energy to every part of your body, mind, and spirit. However, if one of your chakras is too open and spinning too quickly, or if it is closed and moving slowly, your health will suffer. By learning about the seven chakras, you can become more in tune with the natural energy cycles of your body. You can use this information to connect physical, emotional and spiritual imbalances with the chakras that empower them. Of course, with those discoveries, you can begin to balance your chakras and live a healthy and harmonious life. They all play intricate parts separately, but when aligned work like a well-tuned violin playing the most beautiful song. Your sacral chakra is also associated with the color orange. It enhances sensuality and intimacy as well as promoting creativity and self-expression, feeling the outer and inner worlds and creating fantasies. Your sacral chakra is the home of the creative life force energy that helps you enjoy your life here on

Earth. It's the energy that motivates you to enjoy the fruits of your labor including indulging in pleasurable activities like sex. When this chakra is overactive, or even underactive, we face things like addiction and gluttony. Pleasure is a good thing, and you should never feel guilty for enjoying the good things life has to offer. However, if you find yourself enjoying things that are not nourishing for your soul or healthy for you, then your sacral chakra falls out of balance. You end up with symptoms like hormonal imbalances, restlessness, decreased sex drive, lack of passion, depression, lack of creativity, obesity and addiction. It took me understanding how chakras worked to unblock my sexual desires and be free. This wasn't an overnight fix. This took me listening to women and their experiences of different ways on how to increase awareness of self and love. All we really have to do is enjoy life. Be creative, eat healthier and make love not just to a partner, but also with yourself.

One way I found really intriguing was learning about yoni steaming. Yoni steaming is an ancient wellness practice that involves steaming your vagina with organic herbs. The steam increases blood circulation, helps menstrual cramps, increases fertility, removes toxins, relaxes your body and calms the mind. Legend has it that yoni steaming was used on women after their cycles to let the husband know their wife was pure again and allowed to return home. They would send the woman away while on her cycle because they thought it was witchcraft and she was possessed. Straight craziness.

So I tried this yoni steam thing all the ladies were raving about. I heated up a pot with a variety of mixed herbs like marshmallow root, rose, lavender, mugwort, lemongrass, calendula, red raspberry leaf, rosemary and yarrow. I poured a glass for myself to drink (drinking helps healing from the inside as well) and poured the rest in a bowl. I grabbed a notebook, some colored pens, dimmed the lights, lit some candles and set the mood with calming music. I placed the tea in a bucket with a specially made seat to sit over it, got naked from the waist down, wrapped myself in a big fuzzy blanket to keep the steam in, and sat.

Then I journaled. I never really journaled until then. I wrote about how the steam was hot yet pleasant. How it smelled and tasted. I talked about the things I wished to get out of that moment, like forgiveness of my ex. Forgiveness of myself for the abortion I had. How I wanted to rid myself of the fibroids that bothered me. I wrote until my hand got tired. Then I sat there. I closed my eyes, took deep breaths and repeated, "I forgive you, please forgive me, I'm sorry." This gave me peace. I needed that. I sat there for about an hour, got up and it felt like I peed on myself from the sweating that took place. I put on my pajamas and went to bed. I slept like a baby that night.

From that moment, I knew I needed to include this in my self-care self-love regiment. I told everyone about it. People thought I was crazy, but I didn't care. I knew the effect it had on me, and I couldn't just keep this to myself. Now you hear about it more and more, and even celebrities have given their two-cents. After my first steam, my vagina and I had a better understanding. I talked to her in the mirror and started showing her love like never before. I respected her, and she gave me my powers back. When we were little, we were taught to not play with our vaginas. Hands don't belong down there. Parents give it cute names like 'Your Little Friend' or 'Muffin' or 'PomPom', whatever you named it. We never called it what it is. A vagina, pussy, or yoni. We were afraid to use it because it was something we didn't talk about until our period showed up, and even then, we were taught that our bodies were gross. We teach children to ignore what your body does and what your body looks like. Children are curious creatures. Why can't they explore? When we take that away from them, it actually hinders their mental development and as adults, they don't know what to do with their bodies. That's how children become adults who become aggressive, sexually overstimulated and forceful because they don't have a clue as to why certain feelings come up when they see the opposite sex, or what's really happening to their own bodies. They are in such a confused state they just want to scream but have no way of releasing what's inside of them. Hella taboo. Why is sexual desire, sexual feelings and intimacy so hush hush? How can we love us when we don't even know us? We never explored our bodies, masturbation was a big no-no, and we would never get caught looking at our vaginas in the mirror unless we were learning how to insert a tampon, and even then, you were frowned on. Showing your sexuality made you promiscuous. People called you a whore or a slut, so you shamed yourself and left your body to the wind. Now that you are older you don't understand your sexuality. You're afraid to embrace your desires and even if you wanted to, you don't even know where to start. I have an answer, so here is how. You start by holding up the mirror to your vagina and saying hello.

My vagina and I are close now. I ask her if she's ok and she responds. She lets me know when she wants attention or when she's sad. I listen to her more intently now because she deserves it. My self-love keeps me sane and makes my vagina work better than when I was in my twenties. It ain't broken anymore.

Women hit their sexual peak later in life because this is when we finally find ourselves. We become happy with who we are, we aren't afraid to be the vagina explorer that we tried to be when we were little. There is no one around to stop you. Finding a self-love routine that you can commit to is key to your sanity. Understanding your body is the first step to knowing who you are, what you like and dislike and how to please yourself. We are so used to pleasing the world that we forget to please ourselves.

That stops today. I want you to pick up that mirror and just first start by looking at your face for five minutes. Don't look away. If you feel the need to cry, do that, but keep looking at your reflection. Once you master this and are OK with it, I want you to stand in the mirror completely naked. Look at all your imperfections. Each lump, bump, crevice, mole, spot, and hair. Find peace in what God has blessed you with. When comfortable I want you to clean your house naked, in sexy shoes. This is a confidence builder. If you can strut your stuff alone and not feel awkward, you can hold your head high fully clothed, and your confidence will skyrocket. Now we are moving on to looking at your vagina in the mirror. I want you to touch it, feel the layers of what you are made of. Explore yourself and see what you find. Your hands are your best tools for pointing out where your erogenous zones are located. Playtime! This will feel weird, but once you become more self-aware, the more pleasurable your life will be and the more love for self you will explore. You learn to put yourself first and not on the back burner. It took me some trial and error throughout life to find what pleased me. I'm so much happier now, I'm freer with my body, I'm able to communicate what I love and what I don't. My vagina is on cloud nine. Thank you for listening, and I hope you and your vagina become best friends again.

Lessons Learned and Mindset Tips

Lessons Learned:

1. I learned that for others to love me, I must first love myself.

2. You can build a brick wall and block people, or you can build a path to walk on with those you love by your side.

3. Having an intimate relationship with yourself is the roadmap you give to others to follow for your personal pleasure.

Mindset Tips:

1. Be open to change. Don't let the old ways of dealing with life hold you back.

2. Reconnect with 'self'. Tell yourself that you are beautiful and mean it. Love yourself and hold yourself higher than you hold everyone else.

3. Forgive yourself so you can have a fresh start and find out who you truly are.

Aha Moments and Self-Reflections

Note your Thoughts

_____

_____

_____

_____

_____

_____

_____

_____

_____

_____

_____

_____

_____

_____

_____

_____

_____

_____

_____

_____

_____

_____

Rosalyn Fung

Rosalyn Fung is a self-love, life, and business coach who helps female entrepreneurs break-free from 'not enough' syndrome so that they do not sabotage their lives and businesses. Rosalyn is very passionate about helping entrepreneurs share their gifts and passions for creating deeper, positive impact in this world.

Having a background as a registered psychologist and holding a 2nd degree blackbelt in karate, she knows what it takes to develop a mindset to successfully achieve your goals in life and business.

Living a life of love, inspiration, passion, fulfillment and joy through connection and learning is her mode of expression.

Rosalyn knows that your mindset and overall relationship with yourself has a direct impact on the success of your life and business.

She lives with her husband and two beautiful sons in Edmonton, Alberta, Canada. They love traveling, hiking, and giving back to the community.

Find Rosalyn online:
www.rosalynfung.com
https://www.facebook.com/wonderwomancoach/
www.instagram.com/wonderwomancoach

Chapter 6

Unleashing My Inner Wonder Woman

By Rosalyn Fung

Imagine me naked. OK, almost naked...just wearing an itty-bitty black string bikini. Tanned and greased up.

I'm standing on a stage, my muscles flexing and popping as I'm doing my quarter turn poses in front of the panel of judges.

There are hundreds in the audience. I'm wearing number seventy-two.

I'm standing there, showing off my 'perfect' fitness model bodybuilding physique, paired with a smile that hides the pain. The pain of enduring months of severe dieting and uncertainty and anxiety about whether the judges would think I'm 'good enough' to place in this figure bodybuilding competition. This was the nature of the game. We are there to look our best, not necessarily to *feel* our best.

How often are you more worried about what you look like when you're feeling trapped on the inside?

How often is your confidence heavily reliant on how you look?

We live in a world so hyper-focused on *image* and *weight*.

So, my aha moment occurred when I realized that after ten years of dieting to chase this perfect body, I didn't actually achieve the happiness and peace inside that I hoped to have.

This is my story—it's *our* story.

Flashback to 1991, when my parents decided to put me in an etiquette workshop for girls and the teacher pointed out that a little protruding belly on my nine-year-old body was wrong, as I stood in front of my peers. Shame and embarrassment flushed over me as I stood shaking in front of a group of girls my age—I was speechless.

Shortly after this incident, Jeff, the boy sitting beside me in class, told me that Carla, the most popular girl in our grade, said I was the ugliest girl in grade four.

Then there was the time when I was proud of myself for getting an 80% on my math test—only to be met with, "What happened to the other 20%?" when I showed my parents.

These were only a few examples of the experiences I had growing up as a young girl. I was confident, happy, artistic, athletic, smart, carefree—or I perceived myself that way—until the outside world told me differently.

I got messages that I was not pretty enough, skinny enough or smart enough...and after a while, I began to believe those messages. I learned that I was not enough.

To compensate for not being enough, I started to become an overachiever, a perfectionist and I developed a type-A personality. I would constantly beat myself up until I achieved my goals, and even then, it wasn't good enough. I was never satisfied.

When I was eighteen years old, my boyfriend was drooling over a cardboard life-size cutout of Britney Spears, who had the 'Hollywood hot body' at the time. I was so insecure that I immediately compared my body to this stupid life-size cardboard cutout and felt like I didn't measure up.

I made it my mission to get the perfect body, through dieting and bodybuilding, so I too could feel worthy.

You know what happens when shame and dieting come together? It's a formula for an eating disorder. My preferred method of disordered eating was binging. I would restrict my food intake to ensure I stayed in my low-calorie range. Then on cheat days, I would binge on every single food I could think of that diets didn't allow me to eat—including foods that I didn't care much for! Afterward, I would feel guilty, beat myself up for not having enough willpower, and punish myself by doing hours of cardio.

Then in 2008, I decided to take it to the next level and pushed my body to compete in a figure bodybuilding show.

It was at that moment on stage with that 'perfect body', as I was posing in front of the judges and audience, that I realized that my life had come to be so narrow, so rigid, and empty. It was a real reflection that my *drive* to be good enough, pretty enough and smart enough so that I can finally live a fucking happy life—was a *total failure*.

I realized that at that point in my life I was a high-performance successful woman. On the outside, I looked like I had my shit together, that I was happy and confident. I was a karate instructor, a role model for kids, teens and adults that I taught. I had an amazing new husband, and I was a new psychologist in a budding private practice. Despite all my successes, I did not feel truly fulfilled, and I couldn't understand why.

Shortly after my breakdown, I was introduced to learn about a powerful, transformative method called Hakomi.

Hakomi means how I stand in my relationship with myself, and how I stand in my relationships with others. It is an incredibly life-changing method that combines psychology, neuroscience, and spirituality to resolve any issue in your life.

Of course, as a therapist learning about something new, I was faced with working through my own limiting core beliefs.

Through my own self-work in Hakomi, I discovered that I unconsciously believed that I was valued in what I was *doing*, rather than what I was *being*—and what I was doing was never enough.

At the core of it all, although I was highly confident, I lacked self-worth. Confidence and self-worth, which are often mistaken for the same concept, are two different things. Confidence is about believing in your abilities whereas self-worth is how you value yourself. They do not always go hand in hand.

All this time, I was unconsciously driven to do more, be more and have more just so that I could be 'happy' and fulfilled.

As I did my own self-work on changing my limiting core beliefs, I learned how to build my own self-worth. I transformed from thinking I was not good enough to knowing and claiming my power and truth that I am enough.

I started showing up in my own relationship with myself differently. I learned the beauty of stillness and coming home to myself. I learned to truly value myself and love myself. As a result, I started showing up in the world differently.

I embraced being perfectly imperfect. I stopped being so rigid with food and learned to have more flexibility. I started to love my body just as it was, shifting from focusing on what it looked like to honoring my body for what it does for me.

Hakomi deepened my relationship with myself and the work I did with my clients. It was so life-changing that it was a no-brainer to become certified as a Hakomi practitioner, and now it is the foundation of my life and how I work with my clients.

Hakomi helped me believe in myself so much that shortly afterward, I went on to become certified as an eating psychology coach, as I realized that I went through my own journey so that I could share my gifts to help others heal their body image and food struggles.

I was also blogging at the time about my own journey so that I could inspire others. I posted a before and after photo of myself. However, they were not your typical before and after photos. My 'before' photo was my bodybuilding physique on stage, and my 'after' photo was me ten months after I gave birth to my first son, so I was softer and curvier.

My atypical before/after journey caught the attention of the Huffington Post, who contacted me to publish my story on their site. This was truly a confirmation from the universe that I was meant to help others love themselves too.

For the following six and a half years, I ran multiple food, body image, and self-love transformational groups for women (and one for men). I worked with teen girls, women and men to help them feel more empowered in their relationship with their food, body, and health. Food and body image issues are just a doorway to deeper aspects of ourselves. At the core of it, my job was to really help people awaken to consciously re-discover their 'diamond self'—the self of pure love and light that we came into this world as, before all the shame and guilt and shit was projected onto us.

In 2014, when I went on maternity leave with my second child, I also joined a group coaching program for speakers who wanted to create a more positive impact. I was part of a community of coaches and business owners from various fields, and my mind was blown with all these new ideas of how I could get my message out there. This led me to become the first registered psychologist in Alberta to trailblaze and create an international online program in food, body image, and self-love. This was no easy feat, there was a lot of red tape that I had to go through since I was in a very regulated profession. I was determined to find a way to make it happen though because I knew that my work would make a difference.

As excited as I was about creating more impact internationally, I was equally frustrated by such a strictly regulated profession. Witnessing my coaching peers making such an amazing impact *and* having freedom with their time, money and location gave me the opportunity to reflect on my own career and whether I wanted to continue as a registered psychologist. As much as I loved being a psychologist, I knew that the strict limitations of being in such a regulated profession were keeping me from living out my biggest vision and dreams, where I could be creating impact and having freedom with time, money and location. I deeply desired to travel more, volunteer more, engage more in play, and especially as a mom of two young boys, I wanted to spend more time with them in their classroom and at home.

At this point, my personal development work and my desire to create a more positive impact motivated me to hire a business coach and start a self-love coaching business on the side.

I soon realized that my passion shifted to working with female entrepreneurs who were getting in their own way. Women often struggle with their self-worth and confidence to put themselves out there whether it is at networking events, speaking on stage, in front of the camera, promoting themselves or charging the true value of their services provided. I also attracted female entrepreneurs who wanted to take their business to the next level but lacked strategy and systems to put into place and were thrown into overwhelm with too many ideas and directions. They lacked clarity and focus and ended up going around in circles like a chicken with its head cut off. Because I had invested so much in my own learning to grow my businesses over the years, I truly felt confident to teach others what I learned and prospered from implementing. As a result, this led me to add business strategist coaching to my services.

My side hustle began to take off quickly, and five months into it, I started to realize that being a therapist no longer aligned with my biggest vision and dreams. Trying to maintain my psychological practice was hindering my ability to grow my coaching business even more. I realized that I needed to take another leap of faith and retire my ten-year successful psychological practice to make more progress to live out my biggest vision and dreams. I believe the seed was planted in my head back in 2014, but I didn't admit to it until 2017.

However, halting my psychological practice didn't happen right away as I wrestled with my inner-critic and fears of letting go. My inner-critic was saying things like, "How can you leave such a successful career and start all over again? Who's going to come see you if you're not covered under benefits? You have a young family, are you sure you can do this? What if you fail?" On and on it went.

Retiring as a psychologist was one of the most difficult journeys I've had to endure in my career. It required me to work through another layer of my own self-worth issues. I did not realize how much of my own identity had been wrapped up in this prestige title of psychologist and the status that came with it. I had to really work through my own grieving process and loss of identity as a psychologist. It was a huge part of not only my identity but my self-image. More than ever, I had to practice what I preach with my own clients to help me tame my own inner-critic.

Finally, about six months after coming to the realization that I needed to retire my psychological profession, I gradually surrendered and turned to my inner-critic and thanked her. After all, she is there to protect me and keep me feeling safe. That's her job. I stepped into my own inner Wonder Woman and had a conversation—OK, *many* conversations—with her. I let her know that I truly believed and trusted in myself and that I had all the resources I needed to ensure I live out my dreams.

I now know that my true calling is to support female entrepreneurs so they can get out of their own way so they can grow their businesses through a combination of the Hakomi method and business strategy coaching. I help them to have a higher level of impact while also creating more freedom with time, money, and location.

I recently rebranded, created a new website, and hosted a relaunch event where I stood on stage in front of one-hundred and fifty women to declare my new platform as a self-love, life, and business coach. I had tears of joy running down my face as I stepped on that stage and shared authentically how I was living my dream at that moment. I didn't know how I was going to get there, but with the guidance of my own coaches, belief in myself and my dreams, and an unstoppable attitude, I did it. I was so touched by all the women in my community that came out to celebrate this day with me. My intention of the event was to bring female entrepreneurs together and drop them into vulnerability, so they could find the courage to connect with each other from this authentic space. This allowed them to share their biggest struggles in business and know they are not alone. I wanted to create a strong sense of community where women can be real, share, inspire, uplift, collaborate and connect with each other.

I was so touched by all the feedback about how these women had breakthroughs at my event, and the connections that were made among them just lit me up like a kid on Christmas day.

This is the start of a new chapter in my book of life.

It hasn't been an easy journey—personally or professionally, but I believe that whenever we are called to step outside of our comfort zone, it's never easy. However, to feel and witness how amazingly rewarding it is to expand my comfort zone and live out my dreams makes it all worthwhile.

I believe that life is an adventure, and if we don't take the opportunities to grow, to create, to expand ourselves, we stay playing small. You are not meant to play small. My wish for you is to choose love over fear. Explore and expand your boundaries in a way that's in alignment with your greatest dreams. Anything is possible when you put your mind to it and take action. I believe in you. You are worthy of living your most abundant and joyful life.

Lessons Learned and Mindset Tips

Lessons Learned:

1. Know that you are valuable and enough as you are. You never have to justify and apologize for who you are.

2. Never apologize for your body shape, size or weight. Work on yourself from the inside out in mind, body, and spirit. Your body will take on the form it's meant to be when you are at peace with yourself.

3. Who you are as a person is not defined by your career, your pant size, your roles in life, the number in your bank account, the size of your home, the clothes you wear and other such material things. Your inner qualities, values, attitude, and character define who you are.

4. True peace and freedom come from having a deeply loving and healthy relationship with yourself.

Mindset Tips:

1. You are enough, and the world needs you to stop playing small—go out there, step outside your comfort zone and play full out.

2. You are always worthy of love, even when you aren't perfect, when you fail, make mistakes, and you're not living the best version of yourself.

3. Let go of pleasing others and be unapologetic about showing up as your authentic self. Life is more delicious, joyful and fulfilling this way.

Aha Moments and Self-Reflections

Note your Thoughts

Corby Furrow

Corby has found her passion as a transformational catalyst. She is an accredited and certified Emotional Freedom Techniques (EFT) practitioner, and certified executive coach and chartered professional of human resources. Her passion is helping people obtain a profound, lasting level of healing. Most of our subconscious beliefs and emotional blocks come from our experiences growing up. When we can see them in a different light, the perspective also changes, and growth happens.

Stepping into the entrepreneurial world was a huge mind shift for Corby after 'leaving' the corporate world. She can't imagine being anywhere else now. Everything happens for a reason, and if Corby hadn't lost her job she wouldn't have found EFT or experienced the profound healing that has since happened. The people, the energy, and the freedom are what life is about. It's embracing the moment, letting go and trusting that there is a plan. Even if you fall, all will be OK.

Find Corby online:
www.radiantcoresolutions.com
www.facebook.com/radiantcoresolutions

Chapter 7

Tap on Your Head They Said

By Corby Furrow

I sat in a room full of people who were tapping on their faces, under their arms and on top of their head. This was supposed to 'heal me'? What the hell had I gotten myself into?

In my world, I am the dependable one, the one who remains calm under pressure, the one who gets stuff done. I am the go-to person; I take care of everyone. For a long time, I didn't feel like that person. It felt foreign, like I was putting on an act. The reliable wise person act gave me a safe place to hide behind. In that room full of people tapping their faces, I was looking for answers, but they didn't seem like they'd be easy to find.

I didn't see myself as smart, beautiful, or capable. I always had a sense of shock when people wanted to spend time with me. As a child, I spent a lot of time on my own because I didn't feel I fit in. Making someone else look good made me feel good, which was my definition of success. I never felt the success for myself.

The only time that I felt free and secure in what I did was when I was playing sports or coaching sports teams, people, and leaders.

In those moments on the field or across the table, I had an inner confidence; this was the one indulgence that I allowed myself to feel. People often asked me for my opinion or advice. I was always happy to help others feel better but never thought to take my own advice.

When I was twenty-one years old, I was hired by the local mine to work in the training and safety department. Lucky for me, over the next twenty-four years I had great managers, coaches and mentors in my life that kept pushing me to improve myself, and I was always happy to accommodate them. When I was offered a raise, I would feel like I was being a burden and ask them if they were sure. Thank goodness for those who laughed it off and approved the raise or the promotion despite my reservations.

Midway through my career, I got divorced. It was a very stressful time. During the early stages of being a single parent, I was offered a position in the human resources department. I saw this as an opportunity to better myself for my family. I was sent on courses, which presented challenges, as it was the first time I left my kids for a whole week. I had to study and write exams, and the whole time I felt incompetent, like I would disappoint my boss, but I knew I had to do it. Despite achieving my HR designation, I still didn't feel 'good enough'. My life had started in a new direction, and it felt good, but I didn't trust that I fit in. I was getting promotions, but as I moved up the food chain, my confidence wavered.

During this growth time, I had struggled with my ex, keeping the peace and raising my kids. I wasn't strong enough to stand up for myself or say what I wanted. I was fiercely protective of my kids and very independent. When I finally had the courage to start dating, I was fortunate enough to meet a man who had total faith in me and I started to have the confidence to stand up for myself.

He was supportive in all aspects; this was very new for me. It took me five years to trust that this was real and genuine, and I finally married him in April of 2014.

A month later, I was offered an opportunity to become human resources director for my company. The new CEO of the company came into my office, sat down and knocked on my desk. "Do you hear that?" he said. "That is opportunity knocking." When he left my office, I felt like crying. I couldn't believe they wanted me. I was afraid to make the move, as it meant leaving small-town Saskatchewan, which I had called home for twenty-four years, but I was ready for new adventures. The company flew me to Edmonton for another interview. I was so grateful, but still in disbelief that they wanted me. I got the job, but this promotion was triggering me in the sense that it had pushed me to the end of my comfort zone on what I could entertain or believe about myself. Part of me was excited about doing this, but I was also terrified. *What if I can't do this? How humiliating.* I felt so much pressure to succeed and I didn't want to disappoint those who kept their faith in me.

I had a transition period to learn what the job entailed, to work with the different work sites and to create a partnership between Canada and the U.S. after a big merger. As the months passed, I soon learned that American and Canadian philosophies are very different. If the American bosses didn't like someone, they just fired them. There's no real governance or equality, it's all about the bottom line. I had already begun to feel like my core values, and the company's were not in alignment. About seven months in, the layoffs began. I was eating, sleeping and breathing my work. I had no balance in my life, working long hours and spending little time with my husband. On a rare holiday, I constantly checked emails and fielded calls. My job had become my existence.

About ten months in, I could see that the HR department was top-heavy, with duplication between the American and Canadian sides. By June, we had significant layoffs. Each day when I left work for home I dreaded losing my job. I wasn't sleeping. I was feeling constantly stressed, and I didn't know any other way to deal with it other than to keep it to myself and suck it up. In my mind, I was a master at keeping it together and not showing 'weakness'.

Then one hot summer day in July 2015 the U.S. heads were visiting the office. I could feel the tension just having them there. I was called into an office where my boss and another were waiting. I had done this so many times, but now it was me on the other side. I knew the prepared speech well; I could feel the shock rising through my body. I just wanted to get out of there. The Canadian boss said he wanted to deliver the news himself because he respected me. He told me that they were restructuring, and he wanted to personally thank me for all the great work I had done on the Canadian side and the help that I had given everyone. It was painful to even listen to him. My mind was racing. I just wanted to get out of there. At that moment, I became the outsider. When you're dismissed from a job you're not allowed to talk with anyone, you just gather your things and leave. I returned to my office, accompanied (so they could get me out fast), my hands shaking. I couldn't even think of what I needed. I grabbed a few personal items then left the building holding what summed up twenty-five years of work.

I got to my car, emotions running high. As I pulled out of the parking lot, my tears started to flow. I was trying to keep it together as I drove. It felt like everyone on the street was watching me. Sobs rumbled through my body, but somehow, I made it home.

I sat on the couch sobbing. My whole world had crashed. Everything I knew was done. Lucky for me, my reliable side kicked in. I gathered contacts and personal files before I was cut off from my former employer's system. Next, it was my severance agreement. I had a week to decide to take it or not. It was a very poorly written offer; a kick in the gut. An offer you would make to a five-year employee, not a twenty-five-year employee. I felt humiliated and enraged. I only later found out that the person drafting the letter didn't even know how long I had worked for the company.

I saw a lawyer and they were ready to take the company on, but all I wanted was to be treated fairly and be done with them. It felt like when I was getting divorced, I just wanted out. I didn't want to raise a fuss. Even though I did the research, I still did not have the confidence to fully ask for what I wanted in severance, but I knew this was my only chance.

I prepared a counter offer. I set up a meeting with the two people who were handling layoffs. Waking back into the office felt like a covert operation. I tried not to make eye contact with anyone. I felt like I had done something wrong by being laid off. In the meeting, I could hardly speak, I was so nervous. My mouth was dry, and the words were choked as they left my throat. I presented my case as best I could and held back tears, but I was shaking. My face was bright red as I exited the elevator. As I was about to leave some of the employees were in the hallway. In my head, I was saying, Shit, shit, shit but they were all very supportive and just wanted to say a proper goodbye.

The following week we settled on a counter offer—not perfect but better than their original offer—and life on the outside began. My world had gone quiet. I had no schedule, no phone, no text messages. No purpose. I had amazing love and support from my friends and family, but I wasn't in a space to fully appreciate and take it in. My world as I knew it had ceased to exist. Who was I? I had no idea. *How do I function without a set schedule?* I wondered. I didn't know many people in Edmonton outside of work as we had only moved a year earlier. I felt isolated. I needed someone, anyone to tell me what to do. I felt so lost. My poor husband didn't know what to do. He is always my rock, but I think I was scaring him.

Uneasiness had settled into me. After twenty-five years, it felt like this was proof I wasn't good enough. I never thought about layoffs as a possibility in my career path. My job was what I did. I thought it would always be there, and being without it meant failure. I was a fake, a fraud, worthless! I was panicked. What was I going to do? What were we going to do? I had no idea. I felt small. I felt uneducated. I always believe everything happens for a reason, but it was hard to see or find a reason this time.

In my panic to find direction, I enrolled in several university classes, because I figured I must need more education. I applied for every job that I could but didn't trust that I could work ever again. I went to job interviews and would bomb them. At best, I could hold it together in the first interview, but when I got to the second, I got scared. I thought they would find out I was worthless and that I didn't know anything. I could feel the energy drain in the room with my dread. They could feel it too. I got the, "Don't call us, we will call you" look.

In between self-loathing and interviews, I went to a conference where I met some significant women and shared with them my layoff story. They were looking for someone with HR experience in their own business. They didn't know me from a hole in the ground, but there they were with open arms, welcoming me to opportunity. I soaked that up like a lost puppy. My brain couldn't figure out why they would do such a thing, but I longed for the connection, so I decided to see where it would go.

At the same time, I was working with an outplacement counselor, whom I worked with previously in my HR role. Now I was experiencing what others went through when they got laid off. She helped me look at options and improved my résumé. Through many discussions and tears, I concluded that I wanted to look into coaching. I had loved the human connections in my HR role. I had been a coach in one form or another for most of my adult life, so she put me in contact with a coach and motivational speaker in Toronto.

I called the speaker up, and she offered me tickets to her live event in Toronto the following weekend. I said I would come, so I got off the phone and immediately booked a flight before the fear and reality that I was flying halfway across the country to do something I had no idea about kicked in. This was not something I normally would do, but my husband was so supportive of my decision.

In Toronto, she spoke of trying to get people to step up and claim their voice. All I could do as I listened was hold back tears and shrink. Terror gripped me at the mere thought of telling my story. I felt so inadequate in that room of people, and it took all my effort to stay. Everyone seemed to have it all together but me; little did I know that half the room felt like I did.

The next evening one of the exhibitors at the event was talking to me about a program called Evolving Freedom, which was all about healing oneself. I had such an energetic pull to this lady and what she was saying. I knew this was why I came to Toronto; I could feel it with every fiber of my being. On the spot, I signed up for the six-month program, which was happening in Toronto. I didn't know exactly what it was or how I was going to make it work, but I just knew had to do it. I called my husband again and told him what was going on. I'm sure he thought I had lost it at this point, but he remained my rock.

One month later I flew back to Toronto for the course. On day one, they showed us how to do Emotional Freedom Techniques (EFT). This is 'tapping' on meridians in the body to relieve stress and 'dis-ease', that caused emotional energy to get stuck in our bodies If I had been in Edmonton, I would have walked out, but since I had nowhere else to go, I stayed. I guess they were right; I did need to tap on my head to heal.

As we got comfortable with the people in the room, we started sharing our stories. One of the ladies spoke about her mother, and out of nowhere, I started bawling. I apologized, feeling very stupid, I never cry in front of others. I thought I had dealt with the feelings of my parents' divorce and my mom leaving. It was so long ago, but here I was right in the middle of all these emotions. We tapped using EFT to move me from crying back to calm. I was able to release a bit of what I was feeling. I felt different. Lighter. I called my husband that evening and said that the course was absolutely the right thing. I was finally dealing with issues and they were really dealt with this time, not disguised and pushed down.

Over the course of the next six months, I worked on many feelings, such as inadequacy and feeling worthless. I worked on my inner child who felt empty, like she had a huge black hole in her torso. It was dark and painful. She (I) had decided at eight years old it was easier to not feel or accept love because then I wouldn't get hurt, that emotions were bad, and that I had to take care of everyone. If I did all of this, then I wouldn't be left again like I felt when my mom left after my parents' divorce. If I was just 'good enough', and took care of everyone, then they would like me.

Through this healing, I became aware of my decision at eight years old that created a lot of my belief system of who I was in the world.

I was afraid to feel sadness, anger or disappointment toward my mom for leaving. She is a very lovely person and my refusal to allow myself to feel anything negative about her was getting in the way of my healing. Once I got to the point that I was responsible for my experiences, my thoughts, and choices, then things started to change. I could feel emotions toward my mom and still love and respect her. I started to see my mom as a person who was dealing with her own childhood traumas, and her actions were a result of being unable to forgive herself and be present for me. I could love her freely now.

The more I healed the clearer my vision of where I wanted my life to go. When I checked the Royal Roads University website, I saw I had one week to get my application in before the deadline for their coaching certificate program closed. I was freaking out trying to get my university transcripts from thirty years ago. I felt embarrassed because I hadn't done well back then. Part of me was still thinking I didn't have enough experience and wasn't good enough to be accepted. However, I *was* accepted, and I started the graduate certificate program in executive coaching in April. I was feeling stressed as I was still finishing my other university classes, the Evolving Freedom program in Toronto and now this coaching program.

I managed to finish two of the three programs by the summer. I was learning more about myself and the beliefs I held that created the life I was living. The more I started coaching people, the more I started seeing that most people feel they aren't good enough and have feelings of worthlessness. I wasn't alone in these feelings. There was some comfort in the fact that I wasn't the only one with these feelings, and a sense of sadness that we all feel this way at some point in our lives. Learning this about people fueled my desire to become a certified EFT practitioner, so that fall I signed up for ten months of training with the National Emotional Freedom Techniques Training Institute.

I now had the tools and resources to help me deal with all the 'negative' emotions that had plagued my life. I felt lighter both mentally and physically; I now knew what it meant to really deal with your issues. As my EFT training was wrapping up and I became a certified EFT practitioner, fear reared its head: my severance was coming to an end. I had all this training but no job and no money. I worked with several coaches who showed me how my lack mentality was getting in the way of abundance and that reality is what we make of it. I was picturing myself crashing and burning. I was ready to fly, yet part of me was still so scared I couldn't take off.

So, I changed my reality.

I had to learn to ask for money for my work because for years my belief was I had to take care of everyone. This belief did not lend itself well to asking for money. I was so uncomfortable at first because to ask for anything meant weakness in my mind. I had to dig into where that belief came from. I found it was a fear of being reliant on other people, which I thought meant weakness. I could do it on my own; I was a survivor. Once I worked through that, I had paying clients.

So much of my life felt like I was in survival mode, just getting by daily. I wasn't fully capable of appreciating all the help and support I did have in my life. When I felt alone, it was because I couldn't let people in. I didn't even know how. In my head, it was OK if I helped, but not OK to ask for help. Finally, I had overcome that.

Through this journey, I now see myself as smart, beautiful and capable. I am worthy, and I love myself unconditionally. I have learned that we are the creators of the life we want. We don't have to pick up other people's beliefs or insecurities, and we can choose the beliefs we want to live with. I am enough just as I am without judgment. Every human on this Earth has their own trauma and beliefs to work through. To love and be loved is really what it is all about.

Lessons Learned and Mindset Tips

Lessons Learned:

1. You need to visit the pain of the past to truly heal and understand where you are in the present.

2. You are enough just as you are, it's OK to look beyond the beliefs that have been bestowed upon you.

3. It is all about love and acceptance, love of self, and others.

Mindset Tips:

1. Your thoughts create your reality, use them wisely.

2. Trust the process and yourself.

3. Take every opportunity for self-reflection and growth.

Aha Moments and Self-Reflections

Note your Thoughts

Nichole Jacobs RDH BS

A devout Catholic, wife, and mother, Nichole Jacobs has lived most of her life in the shadows, where she felt safe. At the age of thirty-five, she decided to step out in the light of the world and inspire others with her amazing story of overcoming difficult life-circumstances and a weakened mindset. Her career as a registered dental hygienist has helped her to get out of her shell and become more extroverted, allowing her to build quality relationships more easily. Her career as an entrepreneur with a health and wellness company has opened doors for her to extend her outreach. Deciding to become a serious entrepreneur, Nichole knew that intense personal development and retrospection was a must! She worked on strengthening her mindset, becoming more vulnerable, and sharing her life's journey with others. Nichole's life-goals of becoming both a rising author and motivational public speaker are culminating this year, 2018, because of her boldness.

Find Nichole online:
nicholejacobsApril23@gmail.com
www.facebook.com/nichole.jacobs.35

Chapter 8

Manifest Your Destiny

By Nichole Jacobs RDH BS

As I sit here typing my story, focusing on gathering my thoughts, recalling my past experiences and where they have brought me today, I can't help but pause and take a moment to just breathe. To take in all that is, and all that I am. All that I will become on this journey by allowing myself to be molded and shaped by my experiences, surroundings, and my creator. At the age of thirty-six, I am becoming delightfully more aware of just how in control of my life I truly am—and that excites me. Realizing that I have my own voice and can make my own decisions. Decisions about who I allow to influence me, especially those in my innermost circle. I am learning to gain inner confidence that is unshakable. I control my destiny. I have a voice. My voice. A voice that will not be taken away. A voice that I refuse to surrender to anyone else.

You see, this is such a profound, awakening experience for me to realize that I speak for myself and only myself, because my entire life, up until about six months ago, I let others speak for me. I let them control my voice. I was to others, what they wanted me to be to them. Someone who was submissive, intimidated, shrinking myself down so that they could feel elevated. I never allowed my inner childhood voice to speak above a meek whisper. If I raised my voice and told others what I wanted, and what I was truly feeling, they may not approve. In fact, they may loudly voice their disapproval of me, put me in the low place I felt I deserved to be, and leave me there. Alone and afraid. For without their approval, I was nothing. I was silent, and that was just the way it was…for over thirty-five years.

Before I can help you to understand where I am today, and where I am going with this, I must take you back. Give you a glimpse into my past, from childhood through to adulthood. Get you to see things from my perspective. The perspective of young Nichole, complete with blue-rimmed glasses too big for her face. Who wore a nervous smile, shaking as she entered her elementary school classroom, each day. Who fell to the back of the line and sat in the furthest corner of the gym bleachers, praying not to be called out, to not have attention brought to her. Bullied by her peers for being awkward and quiet. Shy, scared, lost in the crowd, feeling less-deserving. That was little me for way too long. I did not know my identity.

From an early impressionable age, I took on messages from others that were never intended for me. So many confusing, negative, harmful messages. I was reaching out, grabbing at them, allowing my subconscious to soak them up like a sponge. Burying them so deep, that they unknowingly affected nearly every aspect of my life. From the way I viewed myself, as to how I mistakenly thought others viewed me, to the friendships I made, and so on.

It is way too easy for our subconscious to absorb every message flying around, under the sun. When these negative messages get embedded deep within us, they can cause us to misrepresent who we really are. "Those kids over there are the popular kids. They don't want me around. I have less than them. I'm not as good as them. I'm not valuable unless they think I'm valuable." Most of my life, I never wanted to be seen by others, because I felt that others were going to be quick to dismiss me as unimportant, as a joke to be made. Honestly, I felt that that was just the way my life was meant to be. I did not feel that I deserved to be popular. To be comfortable in a crowd. I was stuck in the notorious cycle of comparison. A cycle that way too many people in our society get stuck in. We are constantly bombarded with images of 'perfect', people, complete with perfect wardrobes, perfect homes, perfect outward appearances, perfect friends, and so on. As a result of these incorrect assumptions of perfectionism, I developed the habit of being a perfectionist. I developed anxiety around trying to do everything just right. Constantly afraid of failure. Terrified of disappointing others, whose eyes held my value and self-worth, or so I thought.

As a result of my low self-image, the few friends that I managed to gather were those who were often controlling, who would belittle me and put me in my place very quickly. I didn't realize just how poorly I was affected by those in my inner-circle. Over the last couple of years, I slowly started standing up for myself to those whom I had once considered my very best friends. I'd had enough! It felt empowering to say, "No, I deserve better than the way you are treating me now." Yet, at the same time, I was crushed inside. I realized I had pushed these people away, never to return. Now I understand that I never pushed them away. They were never there for me to begin with. They were not friends of mine. I remember crying on my kitchen floor after standing my ground with a long-time high school friend, wondering if I'd done the right thing. Would it have been better to have remained silent? To have allowed her to walk all over my feelings to maintain our false friendship?

I had managed to bury my deep subconscious pain and depression until October of 2017. At that time, the box opened, and my inner mess was fully exposed. My tipping point was when I chose to end a toxic friendship with someone dear to me that I respected. She had informed me that I wasn't the "good friend" that she thought I was, yet she still considered me her "friend," and wanted to maintain a friendship. I remember her words to this day, so sharp and painful, upon telling her that I wasn't going to maintain communication with her any longer. She said, "Good luck, Nichole. I feel sorry for you." Upon taking in those dagger-like words, I realized that I felt sorry for me, too. I felt that I had no value, no worth, and nothing to offer. Nothing to offer myself, and nothing to offer my family, whom I love so deeply. I felt like a major burden and started entertaining the idea that everyone would be better off without me. I would wake in the middle of the night having panic attacks. I was scared. How had I gotten to this point? How could one person push me into such deep depression? I felt like Satan himself was stalking me, forcing me to believe lies that I would just never measure up. Thankfully, that is not where the story ended, because the God I serve had bigger plans for me! I will share the important part of my story with you, now!

Choosing to acknowledge that I was in a dark, desperate place was the first step in my recovery and in claiming my own, unique identity. I remember dropping my children off with my mom, looking at them, and feeling like such a failure as their mother, because I thought I was a failure as a human being. As I was driving home, I saw a local church sign that read, "Don't point your finger, reach out your hand." It was upon reading that sign that God spoke to my heart. Telling me, in His comforting, father-like voice, that I needed to reach out my hand for help. That I had value and worth. That my family needed me. As I type this, I cannot help but smile, feeling an overwhelming sense of gratitude and joy. What an amazingly awesome God I serve!

Back to my story at hand. Upon arriving home, I called my husband Brad at work. I told him, in a shaky, honest, ashamed-to-admit voice, that I was experiencing suicidal thoughts. He spoke to me in his caring voice and told me everything was going to be OK. I opened my Facebook Messenger app and saw a message from my friend, Carly Black. Carly and I had met through Facebook in a mommy entrepreneur group, because of a question posted by my friend, and then-network marketing upline, Melanie Ethridge. Melanie had asked in the group about recommendations for a friend who was struggling with mindset issues. I had no idea that Carly would have an instrumental hand in helping me to claim my life. I told her about my anxiety and depression, and she connected me with her mom, Julie Eisenberg, whom she works alongside with, in their company Rivulet. They focus on empowering others to love themselves fully and sort through the mixed messages they received during childhood.

Julie could hear the anxiety in my voice, during our phone consult, as I recounted a terribly vivid memory I had of an incident that happened when I was only two years old. I witnessed domestic violence involving my dad. Almost every day of my life, for as long as I can remember, I have recalled that memory in full-detail. How scared I was. The sound of my cries. The sound of my mother, terrified, holding me close to protect me.

Julie has worked with me since October. She has led me through several life-changing, Emotional Freedom Technique (tapping) sessions. EFT is basically acupuncture without needles. As you recall painful past traumatic events, while tapping on the various acupressure points on the body, you calm the amygdala in the brain, which is responsible for the fight or flight response. You are later able to recall the past events, as simply as describing going to the grocery store to buy a gallon of milk, for example. Even though my traumatic memories are still somewhat present, I have found that they are fading, making them more and more difficult to recall in detail as time goes on. There is little to no emotional attachment to the memories. I am becoming who I was created to be. Alive, confident, and aspiring!

Shortly after beginning my EFT journey and allowing the negativity to clear, giving myself freedom to be released into my potential, I took a leap of faith, and switched network marketing companies. It wasn't by coincidence that I reached out to my friend Kelli Verbosh on Facebook, a fellow network marketer, and confided to her that I was struggling in my current company. I was working through a traditional business model and was having a difficult time in seeing my efforts bring fruition. I had no idea at the time that Kelli had recently switched companies herself. Kelli asked me to look at her new company and see if the opportunity was a match for me. I was hesitant, but I decided to look. It made perfect sense. What I was presented with was a real, tangible way to build a great income all from my phone, utilizing social media the right way. Without having to do coffee shop meetings, home parties, three-way phone calls, and webinars. All ways that I was taught to utilize in my previous, traditional company. Before Kelli presented me with her opportunity, I had almost completely given up on my dream of becoming a successful network marketer and of finding fulfillment through entrepreneurship. My husband had taken on a second job, shortly before our third child, Jordy, was born, to make up for my loss of income where I had cut back from working full-time to part-time. He would sometimes work thirteen days in a row before he would get a day off. I was at home much of the time alone with all three of our children. A situation all too many know about! It seemed all we were doing was working to make others' dreams come true and to make ends meet. To pay an endless stream of bills, sacrificing our time with one another, and being constantly exhausted and stressed. I remember trying to decide if we should spend money we needed on going out to eat as a family (a rare occasion), because the money needed to go toward making car payments and mounting credit card bills instead of entertainment. Entrepreneurship gave me a new sense of what was possible. Being able to create a residual income that would constantly flow in, while allowing me to be with my family more was a refreshing insight. However, not being able to do the coffee shop meetings, parties, webinars, and calls, due to our parental responsibilities and demanding jobs meant my dream was crushed. Snatched away. The reality was almost too much to bear. I was going to have to continue to watch my husband leave us day after day, working so hard to make ends meet. Struggling to figure out what days I could work, according to what days he was off and able to stay home with our kids. Trying to find babysitters, often at the last minute when he was called into work, after I had committed to give my time to employers. We saw end to the madness and exhaustion in sight. However, upon looking into Kelli's company I realized that I could still see my dream come true. I'd no longer have to pull out my calendar, sneak away from my kids to get on the phone and schedule meetings with prospects, etc. Then, I had a choice to make. Do I go with this opportunity, that can transform my family's lives? Or do I stay in my current company so as not to disappoint my uplines, who are friends of mine? The decision made me nauseous, but I joined. The personal growth that I have experienced, as well as the meaningful, positive relationships that I've created and cultivated have been better than any dollar I could ever earn.

As a result of my personal growth and development, the relationships I've created and nurtured through entrepreneurialism, and gaining control over myself and my emotions through EFT, not only is my dream of becoming a successful network marketer coming to fruition, but also my dream of becoming an accomplished writer and public speaker. I've given myself permission to make peace with my past. To forgive myself for trying too hard. To let go of the nonsensical idea that gloom and doom is my only forecast. To love myself enough to own the right to choose who I allow into my life. To influence me. To share my valuable time with. For I have value, my friend. Not because you think I do...but because I know I do. I decide that I do. My future is bright, and it's also bright for those I choose to take along on this journey beside me. I was once attracting who I was. Now, I'm attracting who I really am, apart from the toxicity.

I just recently started working with Julie's daughter, Danielle Eisenberg, of Blank Canvas Meditations. I have had one of four meditation sessions with Danielle, the first one focusing on my core. Through the meditation, I can unplug from my noisy surroundings and focus within. To look inside and discover who I am and what I truly desire for myself. To drown out the noise that is often confusing and pulls me in different directions. To ask myself what it is that I truly want for myself, not what others want for me. Looking into my core, I accept the answers I receive, and I can move forward in a fuller way. Just like writing this chapter, I do not always see a clear step-by-step road in front of me, but I do see my passion. I feel it, I embrace it, and I own it. I allow my passion to fuel me forward, giving permission to be supernaturally guided all the way.

During my first mediation session with Danielle, I felt a profound sense of being. I felt my body become more fully present, in the here and now. I was able to clearly see what it is that I desire for myself, and myself alone. To be a successful writer. It is in writing that I feel truly free to pour out my hidden self before the world. To be truly vulnerable and allow my inner beauty to gleam. I discover realities and new insights about myself, as I am writing. It's as if my subconscious awakens and I can discover my true purpose when I write. I begin writing the first sentence as I take a leap of faith, not knowing where my writing will lead me. I'm often very pleased when I type the last period of the last sentence. I know I am changing and growing every day and writing is one of my many tools.

Six months have passed since I found myself in that terribly desperate and lonely place. Many of my wounds have been healed, and I am allowing myself to be transformed. I am choosing to be brave in an uncertain, yet beautiful world. I am looking beyond my once seemingly limitations and focusing on greater heights. On greater achievements. Achievements that I cannot make on my own, but that require a team of brave entrepreneurs, around me, inspiring me. Encouraging me to fail, learn, and grow. I repeat the process again and again, allowing myself to dispel all that hinders me and grasp on to all that renews me. To fully contribute to my own self and well-being, in which case I will be able to more fully contribute to guiding others and leading them to reach their truest destinies. To help people believe in themselves. To reach for their goals. To see that what they desire is right within their reach. It is only our shortened foresight which gives the disillusion that we must settle for mediocrity.

Words cannot fully express how truly grateful I am for my past. For the wavering emotions and pain that I carried within my body for all the years of my existence. For every experience that I have ever had. For every person that has come into and walked out of my life. Every experience that I have had has molded and shaped me, in some way or another. Without the pain, without the shame, without the doubts and questions, I never would have discovered that I was a creature in need of healing. Healing from God in the form of redemption and renewal. Utilizing prayer as well as other tools that have been gifted to me in various forms such as EFT, meditation, positive affirmations, subliminal messages, writing, public speaking, etc.

I can now move forward and live the life that I am truly created to live. One full of vibrancy and hope. A life full of abundance and gratitude. Not worrying about every little thing that may be lurking around the corner. Controlling who I allow into my life, and the influence they have on me. As I am healing, and becoming more of a positive person, and exhibiting leadership qualities, I am attracting positive people into my life who are also leaders. I see more and more harmful, toxic people leaving my circle. It is true that my vibe is truly attracting my tribe.

I challenge you, no matter who you are, or where you are on life's journey, to take an honest, inward look at yourself. To see all that you possess. To see your potential. To see your value. To see the contribution that you were put here on this Earth to give. To not allow yourself to be a product of an often-harsh environment, with mixed signals flying around rapidly, landing on you and entering your subconscious thoughts, and thus molding your person. I want you to see beyond what is visible on the surface. If you are unclear as to exactly who you truly are, and are meant to be, I encourage you to reach out. I am here to point you toward resources and people which can help you to declutter your inner-self. To discover your purpose, apart from the toxicity you may have allowed to misshapen you. If you are seeking an entrepreneurial path in network marketing, I can help to guide you there, as well.

I believe in you. I believe in all that you are called to be. I believe you do not have to settle for average. I believe you have incomparable strength inside of you, bursting to get out. Strength that will enable you to truly grasp all that life has to offer. I believe no one else can fulfill the purpose that you are meant to carry out. I discovered self-love. Now, I want you to discover self-love, as well.

Lessons Learned and Mindset Tips

Lessons Learned:

1. When that voice of negativity and doubt creeps in, show it the door.

2. Don't compare yourself to others. No one can bring to the table what you alone can.

3. Trust your gut intuition. You know what and who is right for you.

Mindset Tips:

1. Become more aware of all the goodness that surrounds you each day.

2. Build your mindset and beliefs by drawing influencers into your inner-circle, and by reading and listening to personal development books each day.

3. Distance yourself from those who are constantly negative and complaining. They will drag you down with them.

Aha Moments and Self-Reflections

Note your Thoughts

Suzanne LaVoie

Suzanne LaVoie has a master's in social work with a concentration in international and community development from Monmouth University. She has also served in the fields of hospitality, retail/ customer service, and education, including positions of management and training.

She has served as a public speaker at other venues and performs with a drama group which educates about diverse mental health topics. Her literary achievements include being a contributing author for Unsung Heroes: Deconstructing Suicide Through Stories of Triumph compiled by author Kristie Knights, and Suzanne's first novel of a series, Knight Shift. Suzanne has also contributed articles as a guest blogger for The Missing Piece Magazine, Authors Unite, and Global Sisterhood of Empowerment.

Suzanne has a love for travel and currently works as a special projects specialist for Follow It Thru Publishing and as an online trainer for Ashley Training and Consulting.

Find Suzanne online:
www.suzannelavoiewrites.com
https://www.linkedin.com/in/suzanne-lavoie-sammon-a0981162/
https://m.facebook.com/coolwritersuzanne/

Chapter 9

Broken Piece, Risen Peace

By Suzanne LaVoie

A piercing scream. A giant vehicle grille. The eardrum-shattering crunching of metal. Nostrils filled with a sickening smell of burning substances. Darkness.

It was the night of October 2nd, 2000. I was living in the city of Philadelphia at the time due to a year-long project through a disaster-related service program. I was having the time of my life. I loved experiencing city life, riding the trains and buses everywhere, and feeling a sense of awe and excitement that comes with residing in surroundings different from your original ones. I made new friends from diverse states in the country. I was one of a select group of adults chosen to participate in this program, which focused on disaster relief and awareness. We were divided into small groups and assigned to designated shifts. During the month of October, it was my turn for the evening shift, along with two other women and our shift leader. We were on-call to assist at disaster sites, particularly for individuals and families who were displaced by fires. This work was so gratifying for me because I was there serving others who needed loving, compassionate presences on the worst nights of their lives. Someone to see their broken pieces and help them begin to sort out what the next steps were and make some type of sense out of unbelievable loss.

Little did I know, I would be in the same position—just not with a fire.

On the night of October 2nd, one of the women and I were asked to help at and present at a fire safety event. The evening started out like any other night. We were wearing our disaster-related clothing, gathered our materials, drove the program vehicle, and attended the event. The presentation was a success. We left that venue with feelings of accomplishment and gratefulness. We stopped by our program headquarters, checked in with our shift leader, and prepared to go home. Everything was going according to plan.

The woman whom I attended the event with carpooled with me since we lived near each other. During the day shift, we took public transportation, but due to working at night, we used our own cars. It was my turn to drive this week. It was around 10:30 that night when we left the building. It was a beautiful autumn night, and the lights of the Philadelphia skyline were breathtaking. We were driving our regular route to go back to the northeast section of Philly. I was focused on the road ahead and an intersection that I passed through all the time. Green light as indicated. At 10:46 pm, my world, as I knew it, was permanently changed.

After a brief moment of a mental black hole, I found myself in a state of confusion and carnage. I smelled this horrible odor and saw smoke. I realized it was right in front of me. My steering wheel was crushed against my chest, and the mangled airbag (which deployed) was where the smoke was emanating from. My head and left hand were aching. My windshield was a maze of cracks, appearing like a child's coloring squiggly lines. It was at that instant, I had the grisly realization that I was just involved in a car accident. Everything that happened prior to my going dark suddenly hit me like a lightning bolt. What happened next was something I would never wish on anyone, not even my worst bully.

I managed to look over at the passenger side of my car. For one fleeting minute, I forgot my friend was in the car with me. When I looked over, everything around me became like a still shot. My friend was lying back against the seat with her eyes closed, mouth open, glass all over her head and lap, and blood on her leg. The window was completely obliterated with the other car's grille completely filling the void where the glass was. I called out to my friend, and she did not answer.

There are moments in our lives where I believe even the most prolific writer in the world can't even describe in detail what the feelings were at that particular juncture. This was one of those times. Being in the accident was horrible enough, but for a few frozen seconds, I thought my friend was dead. Killed in my vehicle. Desperate, I called her name again and again, and finally she cried out. My worst fear did not happen, thank God. She was hurt, but alive! We both were.

The ironic part of this accident was that it occurred right in front of a police station. Witnesses were flying over to us and telling the police that it wasn't our fault; rather, the other driver ran a red light and smashed into us. I remember getting out of the car and seeing firsthand what happened. We were hit by a huge SUV. There were three young men in that vehicle. I will never forget the look of the one who was driving (one of disbelief and fear). I kept hearing him question if we were OK. I also heard him say that he didn't realize the light was red. I was in such a state of shock that nothing he said even touched me. Nothing that anybody said even registered with me. I was focused on the wreckage; what was left of my shiny candy-apple red Saturn that I loved and took care of. I was focused on how my friend was injured and away from her family in another state. I also noticed how forcefully hard the collision was because my car was through the intersection and up against the curb on the other side. I sat down on that curb next to my friend while tons of first responder vehicles arrived on the scene. What stands out to me is the man who had to tow the car away from the scene. He had a very kind face and leaned down next to me. He explained very gently that he had to tow the car, and that when I was ready, to come to the yard where it would be. I already knew what I saw in his eyes. The car was gone. It was totaled. Just like my life felt at that moment.

The next few weeks were nothing short of hardship, struggle, and loss. I found out the night of the accident that I took the brunt of the injuries, even though the impact was on the passenger side. It was my friend's petite size that saved her from worse physical damage. We were both wearing our seatbelts and most likely would have been dead if we weren't. What impacted me the worst was that I made the unfortunate decision to drive up close to the steering wheel whenever I was in the car. I can't explain why I did that; it was just a habit. When we were hit, the airbag deployed and had nowhere to go, so it literally blew into my chest and shoved me so hard, that I hit my head and my body against the side of the car (the passenger airbag deployed too). My left hand was apparently on the wheel because my thumb was broken. It wasn't until the next day that I discovered my whole chest was every color imaginable. I had a severe concussion. Thank God my rental agent from my apartment building referred me to a wonderful, caring doctor who was my lifesaver during this terrifying ordeal. He oversaw my treatment like I was his child.

To this day, I am so grateful for him and his angelic and dedicated care.

As a former relief worker, I saw and experienced firsthand the emotions that people feel after a disaster strikes. I think of the five stages of grief that Elisabeth Kubler-Ross describes so professionally and sympathetically; I experienced each one of these following the accident. I became stuck in some of them, especially the anger stage. Ironically, the anger wasn't directed so much towards the young driver who caused the accident; I turned it on myself and continued to for years.

The following year was a mass of medical appointments, interventions, and mental health counseling. I was diagnosed with post-traumatic stress disorder, which my therapist believed was already there from previous trauma, but manifested itself after the collision. The consequential losses became like a game of dominoes in the months following—my vehicle was totaled, I had to leave the disaster program early due to the extent of my injuries (more on that to come), loss of income, and my overall feelings of stability and purpose were destroyed. I also experienced major feelings of isolation. I was married at the time, but my then-spouse was not supportive emotionally. In fact, the night of my accident, I wanted him to come to the hospital, but he refused to, saying it was "too late", and he needed sleep. He also refused to call my parents, saying that it was up to me to do that. He couldn't even look at my chest injuries, stating that it bothered him too much to look at them. It *was too much for him to handle*, he said to me. Gee, excuse me for not realizing that my accident was infringing on his life and inconveniencing him. Excuse me for expecting my spouse or anyone to understand, for that matter.

When the first anniversary of the accident arrived, it felt like I was reliving the whole ordeal all over again. I was working in a new job, but not without more difficulties and challenges. For one thing, I was diagnosed with permanent nerve damage all over my body, especially in parts of my back and arms (I was also given the news that my back would develop further complications in the future, including arthritis and degenerative disc disease). The head injury left me with permanent effects. My left thumb received a 95% healing, but it still hurts to this day to move it around. Activities I took for granted as being easy were forever compromised due to the after-effects. Even taking a shower was painful.

On the day of the first anniversary, I was working in a school system, and I was overcome with emotion. No one was really that empathic to my situation, and I went into the faculty bathroom to get myself together. I looked in the mirror and was disgusted at what I was looking at. I wasn't even a 'who' at that point; I was a 'what'. I hated my body and myself. I was a mess of broken pieces that would get tossed in the garbage, or should have been. There were some dark spots on the mirror, and that became an analogy for me. I felt like the smudge on a mirror or an ink spot on a clean white sheet of paper. Just like the messages that were shoved into me throughout early childhood, adolescence, and young adulthood, I felt like I was the cause of every bad thing in my life and deserved the bad shit that dumped itself right in front of me. Instead of scooping it up and tossing it in the trash, I dumped it all over myself and adopted the belief that I was rubbish. This mindset stayed with me for years. There was no self-love; only self-loathing.

It wasn't until I was accepted into a Master of Social Work Program at Monmouth University that a shift in thinking began to emerge. A very dear friend (and my former youth pastor) highly encouraged me to apply, as he knew I had a desire to obtain higher education and believed I would be an excellent social worker. My spouse and I had just separated in 2003 and, as broken as I was, I began rebuilding myself again as a single woman. When my friend suggested this program, I shook my head and stated that it wasn't the right time due to going through a separation/pending divorce. My friend stated that it was the perfect time to go, as I needed a fresh start. He additionally stated I was very intelligent, and that people needed me. I was not used to compliments like that, and his words impacted me. I discussed it with some other close connections in my life, and they were all in agreement with the decision to go back to school. I had no idea how it would work because my life was such a mess personally, physically, emotionally, and financially. I was a very spiritual person, and my pastor friend advocated that God would help provide if I simply believed this was possible for my life. A quote of his that changed my outlook was "In two years, you will be thirty-five. Why not be thirty-five with a master's degree?" I made the decision to pursue it, and I was accepted into the 2004 full-time MSW Program with a concentration in international and community development.

I would love to say that this was the glue for everything that was blasted apart prior to this stage. I would love to say that following graduation, I obtained an amazing job that enabled me to repair all the holes that represented my life. Well, it's just like filling up potholes in a road. No sooner is one pothole removed, and another one rears its ugly head. After a while, the road is filled with all of these plugged-up holes, but is not really fixing the root of the problem. Eventually, the whole road needs fresh paving. My mindset needed new macadam; however, I didn't realize this until the current decade of my forties.

I absolutely thrived in my graduate studies and even took part in some leadership roles. I met amazing men and women (students and faculty) who accepted and believed in me like I never was before. Both of my internships centered around disaster relief, which was wonderful and heartfelt. Following graduation, I was selected to present a paper in Chicago at a global conference on the topic of disasters and mental health. On the surface, it appeared that I had it all together. Underneath was a different story.

During a class in my second semester at Monmouth, the right side of my body started turning blue and went numb. I was rushed to the emergency room. Following a series of testing with multiple specialists, I was diagnosed with fibromyalgia in my third semester. The effects were so bad that I had to finish the rest of my semester at home. When I recovered enough to go back and complete my final semester, my father died of a massive heart attack. I was also being tested for ovarian cancer. I have absolutely no idea where the strength came from to keep going on, but I do believe it was supernatural. I pressed on and graduated magna cum laude. On the day of my graduation, I was missing my father terribly. The day that he died, some of his last words to me were that he was so proud of me and for going for the MSW. He even said that he loved me. I never heard those words much from him throughout my life. After we marched on the stage, we sat down, and for unexplained reasons, there was an empty seat next to me the whole time. No one understood it because no graduate was absent. It was just a weird phenomenon. Later on, I came to find out my mother had an empty seat next to her too. We both knew at that moment that my dad was with us, and his spirit was in those empty seats.

I am convinced that learning to love ourselves is akin to going for an advanced college degree or a trade. It is not an easy process. It takes blood, sweat, and tears. Lots of tears, at least for me, AND LOTS OF TESTING! Academic tests are less tedious than life tests, though. Life tests require daily endurance. Once a test is completed at school, it is handed in, and your part is done. Yes, you are given a grade, and the grade may not be what you were hoping for, but you can study harder for the next one. With life tests, very often we are not given prep time to study. There are no textbooks for a lot of what we are dealt. I have yet to find a textbook that outlines the specifics on how to prepare for leaving your job one evening and getting slammed into by an SUV, which affected your physical body forever. I have yet to find a textbook that dictates how to prepare for domestic violence, or four cancer scares, or losing your father to a heart attack. The point is—THERE ARE NO TEXTBOOKS! There are no scripts. There is no study hall. So many times, life is a pop quiz or test with no time to adequately prepare. The critical aspect here is how we grade ourselves when we are given these tests.

Unlike most academic tests, which assess your knowledge of a particular subject or subjects, life tests evaluate our grit and resilience. How we bounce back after everything we held true is blown to bits like an inner landmine. Will we move forward after the familiar suddenly becomes unrecognizable? Will we have the strength to believe that life can be good again, even though it is not what I originally planned? These are tough questions.

As I was handed out these life tests, I became a harsh grader—on myself. When I was a teacher, I hated to give out low grades because I believed in the potential of all of my students and felt that a D or F was not indicative of who they were truly about. I didn't even like C's! That's why I stipulated that an academic test is more about subject knowledge rather than who a person is about. Life tests are about who you are throughout the process, and we can constantly fail ourselves. We are our own worst critics. We become that stereotypical teacher with the demonic eyes slapping our hands or slamming our desks with a ruler or other tool who shows no mercy. We put the dunce cap on our heads and stand in the corner. The letter F becomes like a scarlet letter emblazoned on our forehead, believing it screams failure to everyone we encounter on our path. Everything in our lives suddenly become little F's just waiting in the wings to attach themselves to our bodies and minds with no room for higher grades. This was me. This was my life.

2016 was the year I had had enough. I was done with the failing grades. I was done with the self-hate. I started to believe that my life could and did matter. God showed me this through my love of writing. I had a dream to write a book and/or be part of a book. Through a social media encounter, I came across a wonderful woman who was compiling a book to do with suicide survival and awareness. I truly do not know what made me reach out to her that day, but some dollop of courage fueled me to do just that. In December of that same year, my chapter was published in her book. One of my dreams was realized. She and the other contributing authors were so encouraging, and because of that experience, the little F's slowly began dropping off me.

Fast forward to spring of 2017, another amazing woman reached out to me via social media. We had briefly spoken a few months before about being part of her book, but the timing was off for me. She never forgot about me, though, which shocked me. I didn't always believe I was worth someone investing that much time into me or my life. Prior to her contacting me, I began writing my own book. I had a vision of a series that reflected my own life in a favorite vacation spot. I had drafted a couple of chapters, and she was very eager to read what I had written. I was already preparing myself for that proverbial F, but she surprised me. She wanted more of what I had written. Was this possible? Could I really write a complete book that was worthy of being published? The answer is yes.

I am close to turning forty-seven as I write this chapter. Some people fear their forties. Some dub it as the middle ages. I call it my resurrection decade. From the broken pieces has sprung a new creation. Was it what I originally planned? No. Would I want to go through all of that again? Hell, no. But can I say it was worth it? Absolutely.

I can honestly say that I love myself today, even the parts that were shattered. Through my pain and struggle, I have been able to help other people in ways that would not have been possible without those experiences. I set out to travel a new road, one without all the visible potholes. I allowed myself to evolve instead of dissolving. I stopped giving myself failing grades. Today I choose A's. Circumstances will not rule me or dictate my life. Divorce, health issues, nerve damage, compromised credit, loss of income are not little F's that will invade my life any longer. They are the broken pieces that I use to become a higher version of myself and help others to do the same. Do I still have rough days? Of course. The difference is I bounce back immediately and accept that there is a lesson to learn and share. Yes, bad has happened to me, but it does not mean that I am bad. I was created for a purpose, or many purposes. I have also accepted that I am a much better person than before the accident. I developed a deeper strength, patience, flexibility, and compassion than I had prior to that October night. I lost a lot, but gained much more in the end.

Broken pieces led to a risen peace for me. I am peaceful with everything, even what hasn't been resolved or makes sense to me. What gives me comfort is that it makes sense to the universe because it will be perfected in love. Today I am a published author and living an amazing life that grew from my brokenness. My publisher took my broken pieces, saw a vision of what I could become, and led me to a brand-new world. Today I am an A, and so are all of you. Believe it and embrace it.

Lessons Learned and Mindset Tips

Lessons Learned:

1. Life changes constantly. We don't necessarily have to like or even love change, but we must accept it as part of our growth as a human being. Once acceptance occurs, change can be viewed as an adventure to embrace rather than an enemy to avoid.

2. Self-love is a choice. We need to choose to love ourselves and build from there. You are your own X marks the spot.

3. Sometimes we search for the perfect path; thinking that there is one thing that will be the answer for us. I believe that life is a series of evolving paths, and if we choose to always look forward and upward, a beautiful, exciting journey awaits us every single day.

Mindset Tips:

1. Don't let anyone or anything stop you from what you are truly meant to do. Part of growth is accepting what your strengths are and focusing solely on them rather than what others think or feel you should be or do. Enjoy YOUR journey!

2. Everything that has happened (the good and not-so-good) has helped you get to this point. Embrace transition as a season of growth and hope. Evolve; don't dissolve.

3. Routes can change. There is something out there for each of us, something worth all the rejections, sacrifices, disappointments, and losses. It may not always come out the way we hoped, but it can be even better than we dared to imagine.

Aha Moments and Self-Reflections

Note your Thoughts

Michelle Katherine Lee

Michelle is a multi-passionate mompreneur who works full-time within the online entrepreneurial coaching space as a high-performance, time management and business strategy coach and consultant to other entrepreneurs. She is also part of one of the fastest growing network marketing teams in the industry. With her background in emergency medicine, finding her niche in promoting health and wellness was an easy transition. Michelle also works with local domestic violence shelters and organizations that protect the identities and help to rehabilitate survivors of domestic violence and human trafficking.

When she is not planning mastermind retreats, working her 'day' job or coaching clients, she spends time with her son and family. Michelle's passion for healthcare has led her down the path to gaining certifications in nutrition, fitness, and leading a higher frequency life.

Find Michelle online:
https://www.facebook.com/michellekatherinelee/
https://www.instagram.com/michellekatherinelee/
www.michellekatherine.com

Chapter 10

The Power of Lip Gloss and Boundaries

By Michelle Katherine Lee

I am a creature of habit. Everything was always planned out and I liked my routine. I ate the same breakfast every day for two years. When I was suddenly disgusted with my everyday oatmeal I knew I had to take a pregnancy test. I'd learn later that day, in the emergency room for a threatened miscarriage, that I was, in fact, five weeks pregnant.

This was not the plan. Being terrified that I wouldn't see my son's fifth birthday was also not part of the plan. Let me explain.

When I took that pregnancy test, I had just finished my grueling medic training, including state boards, and hours upon hours of hospital and fire department ride-alongs. I was working in an urgent care center at the time but had plans on furthering my education in medicine, so I could get back to working in an ER. I loved medicine and thought I would work in the ER for the rest of my life. Emergency medicine was my life. It was something I loved and something I was extremely good at taking care of other people.

This became another opportunity to see the medical world from a patient's angle. That first ER visit wasn't the only complication I'd endure with my pregnancy. I went on modified bed rest and seeing my obstetrician at twenty weeks and full bed rest at thirty weeks. I have some terrible veins so unless the nurses were true pros at drawing blood, I would turn into a pin cushion. One particular day I was stuck six times, then I kindly asked the nurses to let my boyfriend (also a fire-fighter/paramedic) draw the blood. When I went back for another round of bloodwork the girl remembered me, and I just drew my own blood several times after that. No joke.

When I found out I was pregnant, my relationship with my son's father changed. We fought so much. We decided to stay together for a while but spent the majority of my pregnancy living separately. Our relationship was mostly over, and we were later best described as roommates.

My second miscarriage scare came on a workday and I was written up for missing my shift. While I was in my meeting with my #WorstManagerEver, I apologized for missing work. Sort of. I was defiant and pissed off when I said, "I'm really sorry I had internal bleeding and thought I was losing my baby and missed work. Next time I am hemorrhaging I will do it on one of my days off." I gave my two weeks' notice. That was September.

In January, we discovered my father, who had lung and brain tumors in remission, had a tumor on his spinal cord. Because of the condition of my pregnancy, I couldn't be with him and my mother in the hospital. This took being hormonally devastated to epic levels. My doctors were worried about me going into labor and scheduled a C-section. PLOT TWIST. I went into labor a week after my dad's surgery. It was a couple weeks early, but the surgery went well, and I went home with baby Jack.

Jack struggled at nursing from the start. I wrote this off initially as everyone was telling me "it takes time," "every baby is different," and "all babies spit up." It progressively got worse.

He was spitting up more and began sleeping longer. People just kept telling me how lucky I was, how this was totally normal, how I was over-reacting and just being a "new mom." People dismissed me. Worse, I let them. I dismissed me.

I had this gut feeling, I guess it was mother's intuition or the medic in me, but I knew something was wrong. Not just with Jack, but myself too. Before I got pregnant I was a pretty confident person, but the less I felt cared for during my pregnancy the less confident I was about myself. My worth was tied to what others thought of me. I knew something was wrong, but I allowed people's opinions to matter more than my own and began to doubt myself. Until day twenty-nine. I was changing Jack's diaper and he projectile vomited bright green fluid. I knew immediately it was bile and what he had.

I started packing him up at 5:30 am to go to his doctor. I knew this wasn't me being an oversensitive new mom. I wasn't letting anyone talk me out of getting him checked out. I had zero doubt what he had going on, and now that I knew what was happening with him, my worry turned to anger at everyone who kept saying I was an over-reacting hypochondriac.

His doctor saw us first thing and sent us for an ultrasound to "rule out" any issues. In my head I was saying, *Dude, you mean to confirm pyloric stenosis?* I recognized a pediatric patient who needed emergent care. That's what I was trained to do. A few hours later it was confirmed, and we were headed to the children's hospital.

My newborn had surgery at thirty days old. I didn't cry, I was too angry. Angry at my family and angry at myself for not listening to my gut and letting people cause me to doubt myself. I allowed that.

I finally cried after all the grandparents left towards the end of the day of the surgery. I was angry, ashamed and I wasn't about to show my vulnerability to anyone, ask anyone's opinion anymore or take anyone's advice unless it also aligned with what I knew and made the educated decisions concerning my son. This was a major catalyst into what formed my postpartum depression (PPD). I had spent my pregnancy feeling small and belittled at every turn and now I was just mad.

From that moment on I listened to my instincts and became hyper-aware of my son, his behaviors, traits and what was best for him. When it came to Jack I was a mountain lion watching over her cub. As for me, I stopped caring about myself, and it felt like everyone else did too.

Before and after Jack's surgery he needed to stay upright most of the time, so he was always in my arms. This led me to not be able to keep doing some simple things like showering. Showering has always been a major thing for me. It was how I started my day and how I relaxed.

I also stopped eating unless Jack's dad was there to cook. I wasn't sleeping. I wasn't talking to friends. They mostly disappeared when things got rough. I wasn't working on my business. I wasn't working out or spending anytime doing anything for myself. As for my relationship with his dad, we were just co-existing in the same house. My life became isolated and lonely.

I was all Jack all the time. I lost myself—completely.

I remember the day I realized I did in fact have PPD. I was sitting on the couch with Jack in my right arm and the phone in my left yelling at the poor customer service gal about insurance and hospital bills. I eventually cursed this woman out and threw the phone across the room in hysterics. I looked down at my innocent little boy and I knew I needed help. I sought treatment the next day as I knew what I was dealing with. This was six weeks into motherhood. Not exactly the Pinterest plan I had dreamed in my head.

I felt small, like I didn't matter and like a failure. I was a shell of a girl who once was vibrant, funny, confident and self-assured. Part of me was gone and as I struggled to find myself, Jack was still my entire world.

I was working very part-time on my network marketing business, which was social media-based. I had zero clue what I was doing, and I basically excelled at doing it amazingly wrong. Legit—there should be a car program for people who suck the worst at network marketing. My approach was less authentically me and more what I now refer to as being spammy and gross. I felt like a fraud. I posted pictures of Jack and then I was basically screaming in people's faces, "BUY MY SHIT." This isolated me even more as I began losing friends and family started running far away from me. The picture in my head of playdates and laughter and mommy bonding wasn't happening and felt like it never would. I now was taking even worse care of myself. At this point I couldn't do anything right and didn't deserve that happy life I once dreamed of, or so I thought.

At my son's nine-month checkup his doctor said he was doing great but that I was malnourished. Before my pregnancy, I was a healthy 138 lbs. I gained 30 lbs with the pregnancy, and in those nine months since Jack's birth, lost it all and then some. I was 98 lbs. Three months later, in December, I was 92 lbs. I noticed I had lost weight, but it hadn't occurred to me to care. I simply forgot to eat. My horrific lack of care for myself lead to very serious health issues because of my non-existent immune system. I was sick all the time. No exaggeration. This caused a mild heart condition to also become out of control. With my level of deterioration, I was beginning to pass out as often as once a week. I was scared I was going to die.

I was rocking my beautiful baby boy in his unbelievably uncomfortable rocking chair, with the waves of the ocean and lullabies floating gently through the room, and I was crying. Full-blown, surprised I am not waking up my kid, ugly weeping. I begged God to give me a chance at seeing this boy grow up. Begging for a chance to live because I was all he had, and he needed me.

In this immense moment of despair, I was overcome with a warmth and calmness I had never felt before. Like I was being hugged with warmth and love. Believe what you want, but I chose to believe that it was God telling me to keep fighting because he had my back. I took a few deep breaths, stopped crying, put Jack in his crib, and started to map things out. My son and I moved into our own home a week later. His dad, myself and my son have been much better for it, and we co-parent and get along much better now. That was step one on the road to saving my own life.

Step two was taking back some of my time, so I wasn't having constant guilt. I had begun working full-time from home, so I knew I would need to be more structured than ever. This just took a bit to figure out with full-time work and solo parenting. I would always say, "I didn't have time," but eating or sleeping or showering is about making the time and not living in distraction. My days were filled with things that weren't true priorities. I would spend a lot of time scrolling Facebook, or doing mounds of laundry, for example. As a solo parent I knew I had to relinquish some of those things. I first had to figure out how long things were taking me. It was a mind-blowing exercise. For example, going to the grocery store was taking me an hour longer than I realized. I knew I had to get my time back. I got groceries delivered. I enrolled Jack in daycare a few days a week, so I stopped the work/baby guilt rollercoaster. I also planned the commute to take him to daycare, which took an hour, not the thirty minutes I always scheduled for. No wonder I always felt behind. I hired a housekeeper. With my health the way it was, I needed to have a clean home and I knew I didn't have the time to do it. I got back hours a week and I could focus on work when Jack was at school. Our time together was happier quality time and I was getting into a routine and taking steps to take better care of myself.

Things were still rocky, but as well as solo parenting I started a new full-time gig in the same field, just working with a different entrepreneur coach. Using the steps I took above along with using my color-coded planner, I began to re-establish boundaries. I blocked out my time, protected my morning routine, did a Bible study every morning and read personal development books nightly. I had a routine, but then I didn't stick with it.

I was so gung-ho about my new role as the business and operations manager for this incredible online entrepreneur I threw my boundaries way out the window. In three days, I pulled a forty-five-hour stretch of personal development training. I got run down almost immediately and couldn't recover. I kept trying to push through and became more and more run down. While I loved what I was doing, and some things were going amazing, I wasn't giving myself time to just be. I didn't make time to rest/recover, to work out, or to eat. I was always go go go, and basically living off cheese sticks. Eating ten of them counts as a meal, right?

I still couldn't see the problem. I was loving every minute of my new role: being appreciated for my efforts, poured into with love, trust, friendship, and knowing our team was in it together. Life was great. Jack was great. Things were great. However, that rundown feeling lingered. I would get a cold here, a flu there. I compromised my routine to take on more work. It started with a morning of work here or there, until it was no more am or pm routines. I worked from 3 am on.

Any free time was Jack time, but I'd be checking my email, or I was too tired from the hours I was working to do anything fun with him. I didn't want to let anyone down, but by not taking care of myself, that's what happened. I got sick and stayed sick for a solid six months.

I knew it was my body telling me to slow down but I felt I didn't have that option. In all my stubborn and sickly glory, I continued to spiral to the point some friends were getting really worried about my health. One good friend introduced me to some products to help me with my immunity and overall body function. At that point I would have tried anything.

I thought if I took time off to get over being sick, even for a couple days, my team would figure out I wasn't valuable and would realize they didn't need me. I kept pushing harder and harder until I found myself with tonsillitis, a sinus infection, bronchitis, laryngitis, pharyngitis, costochondritis, pneumonia, a torn meniscus and blown back all at the same time. I had been traveling for work for two years, producing events as part of my role, and I was still traveling during this time. I went to an event in January right after these diagnoses. I was still taking the products my friend turned me onto and I noticed some good things, like my hair getting thicker, my nails growing faster, my skin clearing up, and I was sleeping better. However, I was still getting pounded with illnesses.

When I returned from that trip I had zero voice and got the flu and a double ear infection. I was in quarantine at home with 104-degree fever for well over a week. To say this was a wake-up call is an understatement. Now I was pissed. I looked at my son wondering if I going to live to see him in Kindergarten? I could hear him crying for me and not being able to take care of your kid is a knife to the chest. I was thirty-six, my son was three, and I was concerned I wasn't making it another year. I knew I needed to make drastic changes and stick with them this time. My life literally depended on it. My son's wellbeing depended on it.

I'd had a personal breakthrough at the event I hosted in January. While sitting at a bar at 2 am chatting with my close friend and mentor post-event, I figured something out. When I left my ER job, I lost part of my power. Part of my confidence. I let everyone and everything else matter more than I did. In the ER I could shine. When a code was coming into the ER I would go to the bathroom, get some gum, make sure my hair was back and put on lip gloss and I was good to go save that life. When I left the ER I stopped sleeping and eating, let alone wearing lip gloss.

My identity was so wrapped up in being a medic that when that was gone, I was lost. It took three years for me to figure out what happened to that girl who walked tall in the ER and wasn't afraid of anything. The girl who had friends and a love for life. I had lost my confidence, in myself, my appearance, my worth, my everything. I became nothing. It took three years for me to figure out that I was still helping people in my career today. I was helping to save and grow people's businesses, to feed and take care of their families. I wasn't saving lives with my hands anymore, I was doing it with my mind and knowledge.

I knew all the right things I was supposed to do, but I was never consistent because I always, always put something else before me.

More times than not it was something that could have waited. Most things can wait. No one was forcing me to work like I was. It was all me. It was only once I took some responsibility for my life, letting go of long-held anger and resentments, and focused on what I could change that I saw a difference. I saw it in me— how I treated myself and my mindset. It was up to me to save my own damn life.

I went back to the basics: time blocking and my calendar. First thing I blocked in was my sleep—I highlighted that shit in blue. I set a reminder on my phone when it was time to get off the computer and wind down. Next was personal time: an hour each morning and night. Jack time included daycare transport, dinner, bath and night-nights. I also started blocking out time for us to have fun. Then, and only then, did I schedule time for work.

I re-established my boundaries with others, but more importantly with myself. I made things non-negotiable: sleep, rest, Jack time, and me time. I set consequences if I didn't live up to my word that I kept to myself. It was no one else's fault than my own for checking my email when it's an off day. Every email can wait twenty-four hours. If it's something that can't, it wouldn't be sent in an email anyway. It can wait.

I stayed healthy for two months straight. A vast improvement. I had more quality time with my son and my family. I slept up to nine hours a night. I set boundaries with some friends and my team. I am a better leader for setting the expectation that you must have a life. After I started seeing some of the benefits of the health products I had been using and lifestyle changes I implemented, I joined my friend in business and have been marketing that on the side. That business has grown incredibly fast, and I now have the energy to devote more time to building that growing team and helping people live a cleaner life on top of my full-time career, which I love. I care about people's health so being linked to a company that is aligned with my interests and goals just makes sense. I now have a team of over sixty and growing after three months. My passion for health has made this second round with network marketing less stressful this time because one, I am not being spammy and gross, and two, it's aligned with my own personal goals. Helping others make the same health changes is a no-brainer.

The biggest thing is that I am now living my life instead of wasting it. We only get one shot at this and I was wasting it. I deserve a life of health, strength, and joy. My son needs to grow up with a mom who is healthy, strong and happy so he knows what life is supposed to look like. I can't raise my son sick in bed.

All of this happened because I made a choice to forgive myself and a choice to make changes and stick with them. I had setbacks through the years. Having the ability to recognize that, adjust, and get back on course was the biggest game changer. No pity parties or 'I hate myself' parties. Just getting back on track parties. Once you're able to recognize the signs, you can redirect yourself and get back on track. I became hyper-aware of my own body and took its needs just as seriously as I do anyone else's. It took me realizing the sickly wasting away person I was showing up as to say, "Screw this! I am showing up better for my son, my family and friends, my team and damn it, myself." This is a lifelong process and I am just thankful I was gifted a second chance.

Lessons Learned and Mindset Tips

Lessons Learned:

1. The only way you can take care of others is to take care of yourself first. If you are a hot mess and can't get out of bed how do you expect to be able to have a thriving, healthy life and family?

2. Listen to your gut and don't ever let anyone make you doubt your instincts. Learn to meditate and listen to your own body, so you know when you need to adjust, take a break, get more sleep, or when you need a margarita.

3. You have to go through some shit sometimes to realize not just what you want, but what you don't as well.

4. Time blocking is the only way to give the proper focus to your core priorities. No one will ever complete their massive to-do list, so breaking it down to your key drivers for your life and make sure those priorities are blocked out every day.

Mindset Tips:

1. Only you have the power to let others make you feel less than. Don't give anyone the power to take away your badassery.

2. Mistakes are learning opportunities, you only fail when you stop trying, so don't stop, ever.

3. Asking for help doesn't make you weak, it makes you smart. If you ever think, *This would make me seem weak*, ask yourself if you would think that of your best friend if she asked the same thing. Didn't think so. Stop being such a jerk to yourself.

4. Loving yourself is loving your child.

Aha Moments and Self-Reflections

Note your Thoughts

Nadine Hatzitolios McGill

Nadine has worked in the medical, educational and human services fields for thirty years. In that time, her personal transformation enabled her to see that although many women are able to satisfactorily fulfill the requirements of their roles in the workplace, home and community, they are often secretly struggling with the self-esteem to do their work confidently, without vacillation, guilt and the need for constant outside approval.

After decades of trying to affect change on an individual basis in that regard, Nadine has decided to take her efforts to a new level in order to assist women elevate their confidence and belief in themselves.

Her business, HATZ OFF GROUP – HATZ OFF TO SELF ESTEEM, is developed around community. Nadine provides tools, seminars, mastermind groups and events focused on building and maintaining high self-esteem for women who are transforming themselves personally and professionally.

Find Nadine online:
www.hatzoff.ca
www.facebook.com/nadine.hatzitoliosmgill.5
www.linkedin.com/in/nadine-hatzitolios-mcgill-24b16b140/

Chapter 11

Hatz Off to Self-Love

By Nadine Hatzitolios McGill

"Mrs. McGill, Johnny called me fat," whimpered seven-year-old Sarah on the playground. She was a little waif of a thing with a tiny, angular face and long, black hair.

"Are you?" I responded with a matter of fact tone. She looked at me with incredulity and shock.

"What?" You could see her young brain querying. Mine was not the usual response from the adult playground supervisory staff. Normally, the adult would collect Johnny, escort him over to Sarah, ask him if he had indeed called her fat, wait for the quivering 'yes', and then promptly express to him that that wasn't nice, and he needed to apologize.

I remained standing in my supervisor position on the playground and didn't bat an eye.

"What?" Sarah was finally able to answer, still disbelieving. She had fully expected me to rescue her from that mean boy.

"Are you fat?" I repeated.

"N-n-n-n-no,"' she stuttered, wary of what was going to happen next.

"Are you sure?" I asked. Again, a look of incredulity and game-show inquisitiveness loomed on her innocent, angelic face.

"When you look down at your body, do you believe that you are perfect and complete just the way you are, because that is what I see... A perfect young girl, who is talented and smart and just right. Is that what you see, Sarah?"

"Yes!" she said emphatically.

"Well, then I guess it doesn't matter what Johnny says, does it?" I said.

"Nope," she chimed, and off she skipped, not giving Johnny another thought.

I was once a little Sarah, only my issues centered around never feeling good enough to belong, or to have any friends. I was lonely and didn't know what I had to do to make other kids like me. I didn't even like me. Oh, and besides not liking myself and not having any friends, I was continually told by my primary teachers that I was a daydreamer and that I needed to focus. So, I couldn't please anyone.

At home, I craved attention from my parents. Both worked and seemed to have endless lists of chores to do, but in a young child's mind there really is no reason for a lack of attention. As a result of my immature understanding, a belief formed that I had done something wrong and I was just plain not worth their time.

Some would argue that seven is too young to expect a child to have a sense of self, a sense of confidence, but if one end of the spectrum can be true, as was my case, then the other can also be true. I witnessed confidence in my own daughter, who, at the age of four, with her fiery red hair and short, stocky little legs, had no qualms about marching up the street one day to let some older boys on our block know that they better not mess with her brother (he was seven!).

She was born with that chutzpah, and I cultivated it in her every step of the way. I'd be damned if a child of mine was going to feel the meek, spiritless, insignificance that I had. Perhaps some people figure it out faster than others and are adamant about protecting that self-confidence when it is challenged. I hadn't figured it out, and I sure had nothing to hang on to. It took me many, many decades to develop a sense of self, a sense of worth, and a sense of self-love.

Self-love is writing and publishing this chapter. It is exposing who you are and being willing to be vulnerable in order to find your truth. There is no other way.

I was born Nadine Angela Hatzitolios. A great many generations ago, our surname was simply *Tolios*, until one of my ancestors in Greece went on a pilgrimage to the Holy Land. Once that individual returned from Jerusalem, the Christian pilgrimage destination, *Hatzi* was added to signify the journey. *Hatzi* is the Greek derivative of the Arabic *Hadji*, a title given to a Muslim person who has completed the pilgrimage to Mecca. *Hadji* is the participle of the Arabic verb *hajja* which means 'to make the pilgrimage'.

Self-love is honoring your individuality and your ancestry, cultivating and reaping what is authentic for you, and then sewing it into the fabric of your life.

People journey for countless reasons:

Some journey for freedom

Some journey for faith

Some journey for clarity

Some journey for grace

Putting one foot forward moves the other one along

The wanderer's soul trusting naught will go wrong

The path may be rugged, or shallow, or steep

The heart may be light, or saddened and weep

Some journey to strengthen

Some received a sign from above

Some journey for comfort

Some on the way to self-love

Self-love for me, was the longest journey from head, to heart, to self-love.

What I remember from my childhood is dark, damp, and cloudy. Looking back, I feel like I was a different person and that any memories I have were somehow implanted in my brain. It is as if I wasn't really there, so anguished was I, that I chose to forget.

When I was young, I felt empty and lost; struggling to belong; gasping for life's breath. In my child's mind, I questioned if I was supposed to feel like that...dank and depressing, gray and dismal like a foggy day that never ends. Other kids didn't seem to be as sad as I felt. There was a lot of anger, anxiety, and animosity between my parents and I believe their strained relationship was the reason I felt so lost. I felt their pain, and I wanted to help and to comfort them, but I did not know how. They, in their desperation, tried to protect my sisters and me from their difficulties by hiding the issue, but children are extremely sensitive, and they always know. With fifty-four years of life experience now, I can ruminate about my mom and dad, knowing that they did their best with the tools that they had. They loved us dearly, and that is all that matters.

My older sister was in the same grade as me due to our birth dates. I clung to her for dear life as she seemed to know 'what to do' and 'how to be'. I know I irritated the hell out of her, but being a nuisance was better than being alone. She could not have known in her young innocence and shared family pain, how much more terrifying it would have been without her—my rock.

It was not until we were separated in our high school years that the cloud began to lift. My reluctant model and protector was no longer accessible. I was exposed. I had no choice. I had to stand on my own two feet. As the universe dictates, I began to find my flock. I met a new friend who was just as angst-driven as I was. We shared an understanding of being the child of an immigrant, the sibling who felt like it was their responsibility to fix uncomfortable situations at home, and the awkwardness of being offspring of blue-collar parents at a school full of kids from white-collar homes. At first glance, the friendship doesn't seem like it would have been based on positivity, does it? People come into your life for a reason, however, and ours was that of familiarity. No matter how debilitating our circumstances may have been, we understood and supported each other.

With someone accompanying me in my hypervigilant world, I sensed a release from the bondage of unknowingness and loneliness. I felt the budding of a personality and maybe even an acceptance of, or at least an escape from, my parents' angst-ridden circumstance that hung heavy in our house.

With a friend at my side going down a similar path, I began discovering who I was, what I could do, and where I belonged. I went to a private Lutheran high school that cost my parents a fortune. They basically lived paycheque-to-paycheque, but they never seemed to mind the high fees for my schooling, and they always found the money without complaining. To me, it was worth every penny and more. The school had a small enrollment, a dormitory that created a home-like atmosphere, and very dedicated, long-term teachers. These factors created a closeness not many are fortunate to experience in city high schools. It was a family. I wonder if my parents know that their sacrifice, amidst their own chaos, was my salvation? It is often not until we have children of our own that we realize how loving and giving our own parents were. And sometimes, the only way to repay that love is to pass it on to our children. When the day comes that my own kids fully experience what I am talking about, my parents will finally be properly thanked and honored.

Self-love is having the courage to sift through the misunderstandings and fractured relationships to find the nuggets of gold that only your parents could possibly have so lovingly deposited into your veins of wealth.

I found that I actually had some talent. I spent my time in public speaking contests, dance, cheerleading and had a love for languages. I enjoyed learning, was pretty good at academics, and these activities provided a sense of accomplishment for me. I went on to attend university and travel as much as I could afford, to various places in Canada and Europe. Both university and travel presented opportunities for introspection in vastly unique ways. University required uncomfortable self-analysis and lecturers insisted we dredge up and write essays on repressed memories (in case you have not deduced, I studied psychology), whereas traveling commanded a new-found respect for open-mindedness, patience, and an acceptance of other cultures. Equally beneficial for building a trustworthy relationship with myself was the need to keep my wits about me in foreign places, a necessary attentiveness to intuitive intelligence, and the reliance on good old-fashioned common sense. Every experience, good or not-so-good, slowly scaffolded my journey to self-love. I got to encounter the many and varied parts of myself I had no idea existed and test the validity of the beliefs that had to this point, constructed my response to the world.

Self-love is a painstakingly detailed, Olympic level effort, essence-filled labor of love.

It was not until my late thirties that I consciously started intimately knowing myself and began to contemplate who I wanted to be. Thank goodness for epiphanies! Two, in particular, catapulted my ability to really see how I had allowed myself to be blinded by fear based on a complete absence of self-esteem. The first revealed that I had no sense of worth because I was under a spell. I had always been taught to do everything according to what others would think; to act in a manner that would be pleasing to others; to conduct myself in a way that would not draw out displeasure in others, thereby causing embarrassment to my family. What I needed or wanted didn't matter in the least, and therefore I did not matter. I had been taught this by my mother who had likely been taught by her mother, and so on. Until eighty years had passed and dementia had set in, this is how my mother operated. I suddenly grasped that I had not been making any of my own decisions. It was extremely beneficial to remain under that spell as I could then continue to believe I would be accepted. What a perfect place to hide. The gravity of the realization came crashing down on me at the second epiphany.

One afternoon, in my late thirties, I asked my husband what I should do about a certain situation. He looked at me and said, "You're an adult. You decide." The agony of ripping hot wax off the most delicate parts of your body is the only way I can describe the feeling that ensued. I was instantly liberated from the spell that had clouded my personality all those years and simultaneously stripped of any false sense of maturity that I had conjured up for myself, pretending I was an adult. He was right. I had rarely, if ever, made a decision of my own volition, and if I had, it was not without severe vacillation, angst, and guilt.

So it is here, that I dedicate this chapter to my husband of twenty-nine years, John. A man who has so lovingly saved me from physical death during a health crisis, from psychological death by enduring the hypervigilance and anxiety I carried from my childhood into our marriage, and from spiritual death by standing by my side even though he was not sure by whom he was standing at any given moment.

Regarding my mother's struggle that she passed on to me, it was sad to then watch her stifle her personality as she chose to remain under the inherited spell. Currently, dementia supports a lack of inhibition, and her true personality is shining through. My mom is a funny, cute, engaging social butterfly. We saw none of those traits growing up. What a tragedy to live your whole life believing that what others think is more important than your true, authentic expression.

Self-love is not waiting for dementia to give you permission to be yourself.

Incidentally, I still find myself a slave to the spell when I'm not diligent. The spell exists in the form of unnoticed chatter that runs destructively in the recesses of our mind. Do you hear it? It's like a car motor, continuously idling on a cold winter morning while the noise and exhaust is polluting the air, clogging up nature and disturbing the peace. That is the constant din of thoughts, running because they have always run, having commenced early in life at the indoctrination of beliefs. The brain, being the efficient learning tool that it was designed to be, keeps the motor going unless it is consciously shut off and otherwise reprogrammed. The epiphanies I had jolted me out of the incessant trance, creating an opportunity for new programming. I must constantly be on guard, ever-alert for the old beliefs that attempt to re-infiltrate. I must ensure new, more effective thoughts are deliberately downloaded. I must enlist new recruits and allow them to march away from that hostile environment in my mind to a fresh, more hospitable terrain. I must engage consistently in positive self-talk; talk that provides me with encouraging statements to bolster my self-confidence; talk that provides the stepping stones to self-worth and self-esteem.

Self-love is being mindful of and tough with the thoughts that constantly run in the background of your consciousness that no longer serve you.

Due to my re-conditioning, great conflict ensued once I began to know who I was, what I liked, and what I wanted. There I was, exploding to follow my inner intelligence and intuition, wanting to meet my needs, but living in a world where that was apparently not supposed to be my focus. The mental transformation was taking place, but the emotional was manifesting in guilt and shame—a heavy, heavy, burden to bear. Not knowing how to maneuver through the guilt, I continually found myself in situations, particularly places of employment, in which my beliefs and values were not in congruence with those of the institution. The cosmos was pulling me in the direction of living from my values, passions and natural tendencies and my surroundings were dictating that I submit to theirs. The scenario kept playing itself out as I searched for an acceptable way out of the psychological/emotional dilemma.

Self-love is releasing the guilt and shame taken on out of guilt and shame.

I would go home to my family at the end of the workday, broken and sour because it played out thusly: six hours of refusing to be the square peg forced into the round hole; six hours of operating from a precarious perch on everything I uphold, namely authenticity, accountability, integrity, respect for individuality, and coming dangerously close to being pushed into the pit of conformity. Six hours, day after day, of being bold enough to advocate for those I served, while being frowned upon by the powers that be who controlled staff by subtle coercion and, well, let's just call it what it was...bullying. Bullying does not just happen to our children in the schoolyard or in cyberspace. It is a deceptive, crafty tool used by oppressors of all types, cowards, who care little about harmony, innovation, positivity, affirmative action, and genuine concern for fellow man. Don't kid yourself…it is easy to recognize a bully because we have all bullied at one time or another.

Self-love is admitting to and owning the mistakes one has made and correcting the behavior in the future.

What I have found after working thirty years in the medical, educational, and human services fields, is that most people I worked with did not believe they had the power to be themselves. I have not been alone in this struggle. I have just been adamant about getting out of it. Countless people believe that it is futile to be different and to expect they can be influential leaders. Sadly, these people fill roles that require modeling for the younger generations; positions that exist solely to care for those who cannot care for themselves; jobs meant to advocate for the rights of others when they are not even standing up for themselves.

What was completely obvious to me was that I would not survive with my soul intact if I continued to work in those circles any longer.

Self-love is never selling your soul. Love yourself enough to respect, believe in and live by your values and your convictions.

After years of emotional angst and psychological wandering that ended in a life-threatening disease, I saw my way out of the fog. I squeezed through the eye of the needle and came out the other side, liberated like a butterfly. A brush with death lead to an intuitive knowing that if I did not change my circumstance, I would fall back into ill health because I was not honoring myself.

So, I made a decision...I found a coach and I joined his personal growth program. I started listening to my intuition and my body. I dug down deep into my beingness and took an honest look at my skills, abilities, passions, and desires. I decided to launch my own business, and I did it all without money. The funny thing is, when you really want something, the money eventually comes. Lack of funds is no longer an excuse.

I follow my heart, I take one step at a time, and I am finding that things are happening all in due course. Most importantly, I can handle them.

The exhilaration of self-discovery is the realization that all my experiences paved the way to self-love. The activities I enjoy the most—dancing, public speaking, writing—were tools I needed to develop in order to become fearless and reach my potential. Every person placed in my life played a part in my metamorphosis from scared, lost little me, to empowered me.

More profound is the awareness that the ultimate act of self-love is to let go of one's ego, to operate in a plane of gratitude and surrender, humility and presence for it is there that one experiences true self.

Self-love is getting out of your own way, so your natural abilities and passions can morph you into alignment with your values and beliefs and finally, into actionable purpose.

I wrote the following for all of you who suffer in silence, trying to figure out the meaning and worthiness of your life. May you find it through self-love. It will happen. Just allow it.

"...and then I grew wings," the little butterfly announced with an expression of surprise so innocent and pure that it caused the fearful caterpillar to beam with delight. For a moment, he forgot his trepidation and felt himself wishing to feel such exuberance. He even found himself lifting a few of his feet up to test the waters and feel what it would be like to be light as air; to be endowed with such miraculous equipment would indeed change his life. He was giddy with enthusiasm, light-headed almost, to the point where he nearly fell off the tree branch on which the two brethenly creatures were perched.

Reality came crashing down around him, grounding him to the tree on which he lived. As he grasped for a hold on the life limb that was his existence, the forlorn sense of sluggishness that had dominated his life burdened him once more. 'Someday,' he thought, 'someday'.

The little butterfly flitted off, bidding the caterpillar adieu and wishing him a good evening. It was a most natural act, but diminutive and hurtful to the caterpillar who begrudgingly mumbled his goodbyes. He was envious of the butterfly's light-heartedness and gift of flight. "Oh, to be so free. I wish that it were me."

The emotional rollercoaster of the day had made the little caterpillar very tired. He began to drift off to sleep, dreaming of soaring through the air, fluttering about aimlessly, like a feather on the wind. He felt the rush of the air past his face and the excitement of floating on the breeze. The exhilaration he experienced at the new-found view of the world drew a tear to his eye; he jolted awake as pain shot through his extremities. The cause of the pain was unknown to him, and he began to struggle to flee the imperceptible threat. He tugged and flailed, pushed and pulled, and bore down against a film that seemed to be enveloping him. He was fearing for his life when suddenly, he broke free of the clinging substance, and began hurtling toward the ground. In his panic, his tiny limbs started thrashing about, but to his amazement, his little body began to ascend toward the sky. He kept rising, mounting, climbing, higher and higher, defying the very gravity that almost caused him to smash against the earth.

Then with wild astonishment, he realized he was a little caterpillar no more. During his repose, he had transformed into a most majestic monarch butterfly, broad of wing, slender of body, and full of color and grace.

Lessons Learned and Mindset Tips

Lessons Learned:

1. You are never too old to reinvent yourself. Just be sure you are being authentic.

2. The time to choose to show up for YOUR life is NOW. Stop worrying about what other people think.

3. Putting yourself first is not selfish or shameful. It is the only way to learn to love fully.

Mindset Tips:

1. Become aware of the negative thoughts that are running rampant through your head and begin a daily practice to rid yourself of them.

2. Become a warrior for yourself and a model for your children regarding maintaining a positive, loving attitude toward yourself. Being a mentor is the best way to stay true to your purpose.

3. You can conquer negative thoughts. It takes time and persistence though so forgive yourself, forgive yourself, forgive yourself.

Aha Moments and Self-Reflections

Note your Thoughts

Debra Salas

Born in Santa Clara, CA, Debra spent twelve years in San Jose, CA before moving to St. Paul, MN in the spring of 1985.

Debra is the youngest of three children. To escape the grim reality of her childhood, she watched her favorite sitcoms or listened to music in the garage. Debra would listen to her little ladybug record player, roller-skate, and daydream.

Reading and writing became active hobbies. Journaling and poems were the easiest ways for her to express herself.

She moved to Reno, NV in 1997. There Debra would continue to work in early childhood education and hospice care before changing to a career in administration.

Debra loves traveling and continues to live her purpose and keep her dreams alive.

Find Debra online:
debrasalas73@gmail.com
https://www.facebook.com/debs722

Chapter 12

I Was Breathing, But Not Alive

By Debra Salas

Loneliness was something I never wanted anyone to ever feel. I just didn't realize it was something I didn't want to feel. That gnawing feeling of rejection and heart break. It's another form of bleeding. Loneliness is dry blood dripping from your heart. Like tears. Although it's invisible, it can be felt.

I understand now, that they loved only as they knew how. It's a cycle of dysfunction that I had no control over. I tried. I had a voice, but it was never heard. I cried out for attention, but it was completely ignored. It led me down a path of self-loathing and self-destruction.

From birth to three years of age, a child needs to feel comforted. This is an important time in brain development. They need touch. They need to be spoken too. They need love! Did my family never experience this? Were my parents never held lovingly? Were their tears never comforted? From what I grew up hearing, the answer would be no. How can I expect people who were never shown graceful love, know how to give it? But as an eight-year-old, you can't think like that. All you want is someone to care that you exist.

Love, to me, was acknowledging that my existence mattered. I was brought in to this family because mom had a miscarriage a year before me. When she was about six months pregnant she had an argument with my drunk dad, and she lost the baby. Dad felt bad about the incident and told her if they tried to have another baby, he would stop drinking. That's when I was conceived. Dad never stopped drinking though. At least not for another thirty years.

My siblings are older than me, so they have experienced more years with my parents than I did. They know relatives I don't know. In fact, when I attended my grandmother's funeral in 2004, some relatives never knew I was ever born. That may be when I officially realized that my existence was not approved by some family. I was in my thirties, yet some family didn't know I existed. They knew of cousins who were born after me, but I was not mentioned.

My self-hatred came in so many forms. I was so obedient in following dysfunction, that I don't even know where it began or what started first.

My disordered eating was one outlet. I was 200 lbs at the age of eight. I don't believe I carried it well, but I don't think I really cared what I looked like. I loved food as a comfort, and my parents had no time to bother with healthy food. Mom said people had to accept me the way I was, but those words and that mindset was poisonous.

As I got bigger and was teased by family and peers, I tried to think of ways to lose weight. Not just lose weight but lose it fast. I remember seeing a movie on an ABC after school special where the girl would force herself to throw up food she ate. I tried it and then continued to purge for years after until one day, my throat was bleeding from the force. It scared me, so I stopped. I still needed to lose weight though, so my journey to starvation began. It didn't last long because I became anemic, diabetic, and weak. This dangerous outlet would last until I was thirty-two years old. My self-hatred led to a heart condition, digestive problems, and hormonal imbalance.

Cutting was another outlet for my pain. This too, started when I was eight years of age. Unlike most self-harmers, I didn't cut my arms. I would lightly cut my legs and stomach, so no one would see. I didn't cut very deep because I didn't want to see blood. I just wanted physical pain that would override my emotional pain. My cutting lasted over three years then I stopped because I began to feel the physical pain. The blood was too real to me. It was no longer about emotional pain and I was causing damage to my skin.

My self-image wasn't all created by me though. I was reacting to the words spoken to me for so many years. My nana would tell me that I was too ugly and too fat to be her grandchild. My dad and older brother would tell me that no man would ever want me until I was skinny and pretty. Mirrors and cameras would be my enemies during the first forty-one years of my life.

Things in my household were only getting more intense. By 1983, I was ten years old. My dad was an alcoholic, my brother was a drug dealer, and my family was falling apart. Nobody knew anything I was doing. As "the smart one", I was trusted to take care of myself. Even at a very young age.

Yes, I was smart. I was reading by the age of three. At ten years old, I was reading at a high school level. I had straight A's until high school, but this wasn't a celebrated achievement. I received a pat on the back and was instructed to help family members who were not as smart as I was.

An example: My sister is ten years older than me. When I was four years old, my mom had me go with my sister to her friend's house and on dates to make sure she was OK. I had to be my sister's babysitter because I "knew better". My title would always be "smart one". Which meant I had to be able to take care of myself. This title became a curse to me. I would never see intelligence as a blessing. The adults around me would depend on me to make decisions that I was not able to comprehend. This led to co-dependency and the pressure to always have an answer led to anxiety as an adult. It seemed like I had to have answers for everyone's life decisions. I was no longer living my own life. I was living life for everyone else.

My next outlet would begin to appear. Suicidal tendencies. Life was not something I really wanted. I tried some weird methods at first. I tried to drown myself in the bathtub. I stopped because I couldn't breathe. I tried to suffocate myself with a pillow. I stopped because I couldn't breathe. I started to jump in front of moving cars. Then I changed my mind because I was afraid of pain. I drank Metamucil, ate a box of Ex-Lax, and took a few aspirin. All that did was give me severe abdominal pain and chest palpitations. I do believe I almost died, but it was too painful! No matter what methods I tried, pain and blood scared me, so I would stop. I realize now that I didn't really want to die. I just wanted someone to care that I existed.

No one ever knew that I did any of these things. They didn't notice anything I did. What was noticed were the bad situations my dad and siblings were putting us through.

I would finally hit rock bottom in 2014. November 2014, to be exact. After years of denied depression, I had officially lost hope.

I did not believe I needed to live anymore and I couldn't see any future ahead of me. I was forty-one years old and still single and childless. All I had was my aging parents. My life consisted of taking care of them and nothing else. My dreams had died. My hopes of marriage and children had died. A long list of toxic friendships over the years, had caused me to never feel authentically cared for. I had been used by so many and I was so drenched in darkness that I didn't care about pain or blood. Death was my final answer. Nobody wanted me here, so I figured I would leave. I knew God loved me. The plan was to go home to Him.

November 3rd, 2014. My heart breaks as I recall the memories. That was the moment I realized I didn't love myself. I was determined to die. I had accepted that no one cared and my life meant nothing. My parents had their other children. My friends had their own lives and the gentleman I cared about, was in a relationship again. After finding out about his relationship via Facebook, I think I finally snapped. I couldn't deal with another rejection. Another broken heart was not OK.

That wasn't all. I discovered that my mom asked my sister and her son to live with us. This would mean that I not only had to take care of my aging parents, but my schizophrenic sister and her son, (who also had behavioral issues) too. I couldn't handle it.

That Monday morning, I notified my work that I wouldn't be in for the rest of the week. I wrote out my will and suicide letter. I was going to succeed this time. There was nothing anyone could say. I was going to die, and I embraced it. My plan was to go to a parking lot and take three bottles of hydrocodone and Percocet. I had saved the medications from my neck surgery the previous year.

As I was headed to work one last time, I texted my gentleman friend and said, 'Take care'. He immediately texted back, 'Where are you going?' Something inside him knew exactly what my words meant. He threatened to call the police. I told him I was going to work, but I was going to kill myself after I clocked out. He had already guessed that's what I meant. He continued to text all day and called me on my lunch break. He was furiously trying to get me to change my mind. He knew my work schedule, so he called when I clocked out. I ignored the call, but he persisted. Once I got to the parking lot I had chosen, I finally answered the phone. Somehow, he convinced me to come to his apartment, so I wouldn't be alone in death. I informed him that I was going to do this with or without him. I apologized that he was going to be the one to find me, but that was his choosing.

I arrived at the apartment and was explaining to him where to find the suicide note. I gave him instructions on what was needed to be done with my belongings. As I spoke, I heard a knock at the door. I thought, Oh wonderful. The girlfriend is here so they can see me die.

That's not who was there. It was a policeman asking if there was a problem. Unbeknown to me, my friend called 911 and I was about to be put on a 51/50. This is the code for when you are a harm to yourself or others. The policeman was kind and soft spoken. I had no problem being honest with him. When he asked if I still planned to go through with it, I said yes. He told me I needed to go to the hospital to talk to someone. Once the ambulance came, I knew I was no longer in control, but I also felt peace. I felt loved. Someone finally cared enough to help me. Someone finally noticed I was dying. It took forty-one years, but someone finally realized I was breathing but not alive. Those next seventy-two hours were the most meaningful in my life. Just like the Grinch, my heart grew three sizes that day.

I would be kept in the ER on suicide watch for three days because the mental hospital was too full. The nurses took good care of me. I cried because I had never been cared for this way. For once, I was being taken care of. I felt loved.

The 51/50 hold was the biggest lesson I learned in life. I grew from that experience and I learned some valuable lessons. I learned that being a people pleaser is deadly. I learned that I need to be selfish sometimes. In the first few months, I also learned some deep dark truths. I was allowed outpatient counseling, and that tore me to pieces. I had to face everything that caused me to hate myself. I had to revisit the hurts. I had to revisit the rejections. I had to remove not only my mask, but the masks of others in my life. It was a freeing time, but freedom is not "free". I didn't realize I had suppressed so many memories. The facts of why I self-destructed, began to surface...and they were gory ugly facts. I barely could face people who were involved, but I knew I had too. To heal, I had to claw out of the murky dark pit. Accepting that family members were never emotionally or mentally healthy was bittersweet. The facts stung, but truth is never comfortable. I had to face the fact that true love was never expressed. Even harder to accept was the fact that it will never be expressed. Mental illness ran deep in my family. As did addictions and sexual abuse. I was going to need to forgive and love myself and them.

Almost four years have passed, and I have removed a lot of people from my life. I 'detoxed' from dysfunction. I removed myself from family activities for almost two years. I let go of friendships, even long-term ones. Was it easy? Absolutely not! It turned my whole life inside out. I was now alone in certain situations. I didn't have anyone to talk to...except God. That was when I needed Him most. It was the time to be honest.

How did I learn to love myself? What a question. Honestly, the journey to self-acceptance and self-love, has been the darkest, most intense period of my life. There has been more blood, sweat, and tears in this chapter of my life, than any other time. To love myself, I had to know why I hated myself. That meant I had to face the truth about family members and God. In order to love myself, I had to stop worrying about what others think of me. I know it sounds cliché, but it's true. To save my life, I had to accept that some people do not know how to love authentically. I must not wait for anyone's approval. To love myself, I have to be brave and do what I want.

Co-dependency is a sick habit. I would even categorize it as a mental illness, just like depression and anxiety. It leads to unhealthy fears of loneliness. It's a thief! Co-dependency will rob you of joy and peace. It will murder your dreams! Allow yourself to be identified differently. Don't identify yourself by your friends, job, spouse, or family. Decide for yourself what you like! You decide who you are! You choose and don't be afraid to offend!

Learning to love myself meant it was time to see how others loved me and what they had taught me about love. I wasn't taught a healthy way of love. That doesn't mean I wasn't loved. It just means that my family loved me in the only way they knew. My parents were raised by a firmer generation. Love, praise, and acceptance weren't a common theme in their households. Life was just about hard work, and you didn't have to tell family you loved them because they should just automatically know that. After all, it's required, right? Wrong. Never assume that anyone knows how you feel about them. Vocalize your feelings regularly. Hug your partner and your children. Tell them you love them. Tell your friends that you love and appreciate them.

One lesson in loving myself was to look in the mirror without breaking it or turning away. To be honest, this just barely happened. About six months ago, I became friends with the mirror. Same with the camera. I think I have finally accepted both. It was not easy. I cried a lot. It's a daily process.

I had to grow in my faith in God. I had to learn to see Him as my heavenly father. I had to accept some harsh realities to love myself. I had to accept the fact that I may never receive the love I was seeking from my family. I had to find my identity in something more. I had to learn to love my own presence. What I mean is, I had to enjoy my own company. To love yourself, you need to enjoy being alone with yourself. Go out to dinner. Go to a movie. Take a walk...alone. Spend time with yourself. Date yourself. Honestly, we take more time getting to know others than we do ourselves. It's time to change that.

It has been a long road, but mission accomplished! I love my life, meaning, I love that I exist. I have value. I have worth. I have a purpose in this life! Everything I experienced happened for a reason and I don't regret any of it.

I love my family. I forgive my family. I love myself. I forgive myself.

Lessons Learned and Mindset Tips

Lessons Learned:

1. Stop being a people pleaser. You think more of them than they think of you.

2. Instead of self-harm, have self-love. It's not selfish to love yourself.

3. Sometimes, you won't get the approval you are looking for, and that's OK. Move on.

Mindset Tips:

1. Stop looking for the living in the land of the dead. Look for life givers!

2. Forgive yourself first. Love yourself first.

3. Remember, you only have one life to live. You don't want to spend it with a heavy burden.

Aha Moments and Self-Reflections

Note your Thoughts

Shannon Watkins

Shannon Watkins is often called a princess warrior by her friends. When obstacles come her way, she slays them gracefully. While raising her four boys single-handedly, she grew her network marketing business and achieved Millionaire Club status within three years, pulling her family out of poverty and desperation. She is passionate about helping other women find their confidence and discover their purpose in life while learning to DREAM BIGGER with God. Shannon has faced obstacles, trials, and tribulations in the rollercoaster of life but has learned to find joy and a hope that the best is still yet to come. There are still many stories in Shannon's life still being written by the greatest author of all time.

Stay tuned, Shannon is just getting started and intends to live her life to the fullest, leaving nothing unchecked on her bucket list.

Find Shannon online:
www.GodsWarriorPrincess.com
www.instagram.com/fitish_momof4
www.facebook.com/bikiniready

Chapter 13

I Am Enough

By Shannon Watkins

"You have too many freckles."

"Your ears stick out when you wear that dumb ponytail."

"You need to shave your legs. They are SO hairy."

"Yeah, and your face! Look, she has a mustache!"

"And you're so tall. Why? Did you get held back a grade?"

I will never forget the insults that surrounded and engulfed me that first day of second grade, as six girls stood around me and pointed out every 'flaw' they could imagine. Thirty years later, I sat in a psychologist's office crying over that exact memory. I was there for a different reason. I was trying to overcome extreme depression and anxiety brought on by divorce, but my psychologist thought we should start with the childhood teasing. Tears streamed down my face, and suddenly it was hard to breathe as I relived that moment and described it to her in vivid detail.

What she said, as she handed me a fistful of tissues, still blows my mind. "You married a narcissist because you were deeply wounded as a child. You were seeking your worth from a man because you did not know how to get it back yourself after you felt it was stolen from you at a young age. He said things that your soul was hungry for, and you ate it up. He then was able to use and abuse you and keep you coming back for more because you still have not learned to find your own worth."

Ouch. Her words cut right through all my hardened layers of defenses I had so carefully built up over the previous thirty-plus years. That was the first memory I had of being body shamed, but it was definitely not the only time. In fact, as my therapy progressed over the next few weeks, we uncovered several more times that still stung to recall.

"Put that bread back. You don't need more carbs."

"You're certainly bigger than all the other girls your age, aren't you?"

"You'll never find anyone to love you. You're fat and ugly."

"Are you really going to eat all that? Do you think you should?"

Maybe a few of the insults weren't intended to be insults at all, but some were. Perhaps a stronger girl would have brushed it off and not let it eat at her soul. However, those words echoed with me for years and years to come.

I hid under the bleachers to get out of doing P.E. because I didn't want the other girls to laugh at me in the changing room. I wore the baggiest clothes I could find to cover my developing body that seemed to bring me nothing but shame in middle school. I avoided certain crowds and situations and tried to stay in control of anything that could be controlled by me, including my friends. Eventually, I met a guy that said all the right things. He told me I was beautiful and how much he loved me. I needed his words so badly that I ignored all the red flags and even all the warnings from my friends and family not to commit to him. Shortly after turning eighteen, and against everyone else's advice, I married him.

I gave up full scholarships to college to be a wife and worked overtime to provide for our family as I quickly became a mommy. Every day I tried my hardest to be perfect for my husband, to get his approval. Days after having our first son, I got a phone call from a friend telling me about my husband's first affair. I couldn't believe it. I was completely devastated. Everyone told me to leave him, but I stayed. I took on full responsibility for his affair. Had I not been pregnant, had I been skinnier, had I felt better, he wouldn't have cheated. I justified his actions and accepted his flippant apologies and promises to never do it again.

He joined the military and moved us several times across the country to new places, each time leaving family and friends and apparently other affairs behind. Over the years I became more and more isolated, and he used that to his advantage. He no longer tried to hide his behaviors and would even rub it in my face. "If you were a better wife, I wouldn't do these things. You just don't make me happy." Then came the, "If you get any fatter, I will divorce you." I believed him…not just about him leaving me, but about being fat. When I walked in front of a mirror, I no longer saw a size eight with a cute, spiky haircut and beautiful blue eyes. I saw fat rolls and triple chins and arms as big as tree trunks. I saw thighs that overlapped and a butt that sagged. I eventually stopped looking in the mirror and would avoid them at all costs. I became so depressed with my appearance that I refused to eat at buffets out of fear that someone would laugh at me and judge me for eating since I was "so fat." As the remarks and affairs blatantly continued, I struggled to control everything I could with a perfectly clean house. I scrubbed baseboards and fluffed pillows all day long. I obsessed over lines in the carpet and perfectly folded towels. Then after trying to starve myself all day, I would go and eat three or four times the amount that I should…and then go purge it all.

As I got skinnier, I hoped for my husband's approval, but it never came. I would try so hard with my appearance and yet he would comment on other women's looks in front of me and ignore mine completely. Eventually, I had stressed my body and mind out so much that I was in a severe depression. When I sought counseling, I was told that I had body dysmorphic disorder with bulimic tendencies, meaning no matter what the mirror actually showed, I saw something else. I immediately saw all my flaws amplified, some even imagined. I saw an obese woman in the mirror when I was never obese in reality. Thankfully, my therapist recommended natural alternatives and suggested I start with my diet. We worked on treating my body well with food instead of punishing it. She suggested some supplements that had an amazing impact on my mood and depression, and even the body dysmorphic disorder. As I began eating clean, healthy meals, I felt better, and eventually, the bulimia stopped.

Looking back now, I know that the bulimia and BDD were just symptoms of a much larger problem. I began to control how I ate and obsess over the healthy food in much the same way I did the perceived extra fat rolls and the lines in the carpet. I began to find my worth in how many calories I consumed and what I ate (or didn't eat) that day. Still, I longed for my husband to find me worthy.

Shortly after having our third son and yet another move, this time from Washington, DC, to Oklahoma, we found ourselves struggling financially. More depression set in as my healthy meals were a thing of the past, and we had to eat whatever WIC provided. I gained more and more weight, but I refused to go back to my old tendencies. I had come too far for that. I literally lay down on my living room floor, face into the carpet, and sobbed and begged God to do something...to change things for me and my boys. When I was done praying, I logged onto Facebook on my laptop, because that's what we do when we're done praying. Instantly, I saw an ad for a home business based on natural skin care and supplements for weight loss. I knew I wanted the products and I knew if they worked they could make money. The problem was that I was such an extreme introvert, I didn't know if I could sell them. Nevertheless, I was willing to take a risk to improve the way I felt, and the way things were financially for our family.

Things with my husband grew worse as I started my own home business. He constantly made comments about me selling "skinny products" and laughed about them not working. He made fun of the products and me...but I threw myself into the business more and more. I was determined to prove him wrong.

The products did work. I lost weight, I felt great, and I quickly started making money. I dove into self-help books and learned about the industry and the power of mindset. One book that changed my life forever was What to Say When You Talk to Yourself. I learned that I was responsible for the things I was saying to myself and out loud...that my success was dependent on how I felt about MYSELF. The more I worked on positivity and affirming myself, the more my business grew. I even went as far as writing notes to myself on my mirror. Instead of avoiding the mirror, I made myself stand there every morning and read what I had written. I let the words absorb fully into my mind…

"I am fearfully and wonderfully made." A verse from Psalm 139, one of my favorites since I had learned it in the fifth grade. I was not an accident. I was not just a product of human flesh, I was carefully knitted together and designed just the way my creator wanted me.

"I am made in His image. I am a daughter of the king." Romans 8:29. Not only did He create me, but He cares enough to call me His daughter.

"I am beautiful."

"I am good at this business."

"I am a leader."

"I am a good mommy.'

"I am smart."

The list went on and on…for years. My self-esteem grew right alongside my business. I continued to pour myself into my business and become the best that I possibly could. My marriage, however, never improved. After hitting the millionaire's club and being recognized as a top earner for the sixth year in a row, I received a text that shattered my world yet again. My husband was having an affair with my neighbor. It had been going on for six months, and I had been too busy with my business and being a mommy to our four kids to even notice. I showed him the text from the neighbor's husband. He didn't deny it, he just began to pack up his stuff. I stood there watching him load up his BMW that I had paid for and began screaming, "Why was I not enough? I am good enough!"

Over the next few weeks, panic and anxiety were constant as the same words echoed throughout my entire being. "I am enough!" The problem, however, wasn't just that my husband didn't see me as enough…it was that I never believed I was enough. I was never skinny enough, pretty enough, smart enough, strong enough, fast enough, or good enough. I never made enough money…the house was never clean enough. No matter what I did…it was never ENOUGH.

I grabbed a paper towel and erased all my affirmations from my mirror…gone was the "I am a top leader. I will make $50,000 a month." In its place was a simple, "I AM ENOUGH."

I stood there and sobbed as the words began to sink into my mind. It had to start with me. Everything was out of control and for the first time ever, I didn't want to be in control. I wanted to be OK just the way I was…broken, imperfect and poured out. I wanted to truly be enough for myself, my kids, and whoever came into my life just the way I was.

I set out on a journey that day to be happy…to learn to love myself. I called a psychologist that came highly recommended, and I sat in her office for several hours a week. We started back with that day in second grade, the day I started to believe that I wasn't enough. We worked through feelings and memories and beliefs.

I remember her asking me, "Who are you? What makes you…you?" I remember staring at her blankly before stating, "Well, I am a mom of four boys. I was a wife, but now I'm not. I'm a top leader in my network marketing company, and well…"

She sat waiting for me to continue but I didn't. After a long silence, she said, "Tell me five amazing things about you."

When again I sat in silence, she said, let's start here. "The people that love you. What would they say about you? What do you love to do? What makes your face light up? What makes you laugh till you cry? What can you not live without? What's the one thing a day you don't want to miss out on?"

I had no answers for her. I knew my friends would say I had a big heart and that I gave generously. I didn't know if I even believed that because I saw myself as selfish for wanting to pursue more and more money with my career. I had no clue beyond that how my friends felt about me. I had nothing that I loved to do, all I did was work and clean and try harder. My children made my face light up—when I wasn't too busy with other things. Nothing made me laugh till I cried…in fact, I didn't remember ever laughing, at least not in years and years. The one thing a day I don't want to miss out on? I already was…my children's lives.

She wrote the questions down and handed them to me. She then told me my assignment was to come back to the next appointment with a list of things that I love and a list of things in my life that I don't enjoy that I'm doing anyway. She explained that I had to experiment with new things over the weekend to figure out what I enjoyed. My other assignment was to schedule two hours a day of 'me time'.

I am pretty sure I did laugh at that one a little as she knew I was a single mom of four boys.

I did as I was told. I took her assignment and continued it not just over the weekend but over the following few months. I didn't just want to 'find myself', I wanted to create the person I wanted to be since all of my adult life had been spent trying to be who someone else wanted me to be.

I started the journey by loading up my four precious boys and heading out on a spring break trip to an amusement park in the Ozark mountains. Our family had been going there for years, and it was a place I knew that we could relax and have fun together. In this park, they have a children's area with a giant ball pit. Cannons fire foam balls in all directions and buckets are filled and dumped on top of innocent bystanders' heads as they watch the foam ball battles.

Every year that we had gone to this park, I sat and watched my children play. If they begged me to play with them I would usually make a lame excuse and continue working on my phone, pausing only to snap a picture of their fun.

This time, when a ball smacked me in the side of the head, I laughed, put down my phone, and returned fire of all the balls I could gather. Before long, my children and I were laughing so hard I could barely breathe.

When I returned home, I wanted to continue to laugh, so I started attending comedy clubs and local improv shows with friends. I also made sure to be intentional with putting down my phone and being present with my children.

I started saying yes to things I always said no to before. I said yes to trying new foods, new restaurants, and hanging out with new friends.

For my me time, she recommended physical exercise to help with the depression. I thought I hated exercise, but I tried it anyway because it was for a greater purpose. Surprisingly, by the third day of doing Pilates, I learned that I love to work out and I love Pilates. I enthusiastically cleaned out my ex-husband's man cave, sold his pool table, and created my own home gym. My work out quickly became one of the daily things I never wanted to miss. I didn't do it to punish my body, but because of how it made me feel. Working out makes me feel strong, powerful, in control of my body, and healthy. I do it happily because I love my body.

I also learned that bubble baths and candlelight are essential (at least once a week), and a good massage is well worth the money in the budget because I was a much better mommy afterward. I learned that I love to journal. Nowadays my two hours of me time is split between my workout, my journaling and simply reading my Bible. I learned that I hate cleaning the house. However, I also learned that true friends don't care if there are lines in the carpet, if the pillows are fluffed and turned the right way, or even if there are (a few) dishes in the sink. (I keep my house decently clean, but please don't lick the floors, since they are no longer clean enough for that. Also, please don't look behind the couch cushions or inside the closets.) I learned that I really do enjoy working on my business and doing personal development, but on a schedule…with my boys taking a priority. I also learned I love tattoos and sometimes they work better than the affirmations on the mirror, and I have since added three affirmations to my body that I see every single day. I love turquoise and purple, and tacos are my favorite food.

I learned that my true worth does not change based on some other person's ability to see it. It does not go up or down based on how much makeup I have on or what size jeans I am wearing. It did not fluctuate one ounce when my husband cheated on me, or even when he left me. I was worthy, simply because God loves me. My worth was not based on me, but what someone else had already paid for me.

During this time, a dear friend told me a story of two precious gems. She told me that one was owned by a king who loved his gem so much he put it in a locked case and admired it every day.

He would show it off to his guests and brag about its beauty. The other gem ended up in the hands of a beggar. Desperate for food and addicted to drugs, the beggar immediately traded the gem for a quick fix and a loaf of bread. She went on to explain to me that the gems were both precious, appraised at the same value and the gem's value never changed based on their owner's inability to see their worth.

Just like that gem, I realized I am precious. My value didn't change whether I was displayed as a trophy wife or discarded and replaced with the neighbor's wife.

Every day was a journey of believing that the things I had been through and the things that had been said about me did not make me…me. Every day I had to strive to become who I wanted to be. Every day I had to fill my mind with positivity, affirmation, and scriptures. Every day I had to surround myself with people who believed in me, who rooted for me, and who held me accountable to be who I said I wanted to be.

Eventually, the day came when I sat in the psychologist's office, pushed the tissues back across the table toward her, and said, "I don't need them." Nothing anyone ever said about me makes me, me. Some other human being's opinion of me does not make me more or less me. I realized something… I am enough. I am enough for God, and I am enough for me. God really loves me, and I really love me. On the days that I don't feel like I'm enough, my God says, "I Am.'"

Lessons Learned and Mindset Tips

Lessons Learned:

1. Your worth does not change because of someone's inability to value you. You are valuable just because you are YOU. When you know your worth, others will see it.

2. Happiness is possible. It starts within you and may require a lot of work to reinvent yourself and your surroundings. No one is responsible for making YOU happy...except you.

3. Your job is not to make someone else happy. Your job is to be happy and the right people will be happy because they get to be with you.

Mindset Tips:

1. Start believing about yourself what you want others to see. Write yourself affirmations on the mirror or on post it notes. Send yourself reminders on your phone that you are worthy, capable, and enough.

2. Realize that sometimes it's OK to not be OK. Rock bottom can be the start of something new and beautiful, but you must get up and use the dirt being thrown in the pit to climb on. Do not lie down and stay there, you will get buried.

3. Write a list of who you want to be. What makes you...YOU? What would make you the happiest you could ever be? Turn that into an action plan.

4. Figure out what you love and reinvent your life to match.

Aha Moments and Self-Reflections

Note your Thoughts

Carine Werner

Carine makes a difference in peoples' lives, by causing miracles and being a source of power that creates self-love, joy and success. She believes every one of us has a gift that can make a difference somewhere and to someone. Carine teaches people to generate success in their businesses and life by using the power of self-love as fuel.

As an entrepreneur, using her passion and talents, Carine leveraged her knowledge to grow multiple six-figure income from nothing. She used key mindset strategies and actionable tools to create time and financial freedom.

Carine is an author, speaker and mentor who changes lives. She lives in Arizona with her husband Matt and their three children.

Find Carine online:
www.facebook.com/askcarine
www.instagram.com/askcarine
www.askcarine.com

Chapter 14

Spark Your Joy

By Carine Werner

The truth is self-love has everything to do with it. As a young girl I was lost and couldn't begin to have an ounce of self-love or even know what that was. I remember looking around always wishing I was more like someone else in my class. I always wanted what others had, whether it was their clothes, their looks or their lifestyle.

It was a painful way to go through life.

Then came a pivotal year in my life, I embarked on a personal development journey. I invested in myself and took seminars. I worked with coaches to shed the insecurities and the beliefs that I was not good enough, a recurring theme that kept popping into my head repeatedly.

Here is what I have learned: our inner dialog and personal affirmations go hand in hand and will either make or break us. Learning the tools and skills for self-love and a mindset to support it is key. I will teach an affirmation formula later in this chapter that will support you in achieving your highest and wildest wishes and dreams.

What I found to be the core feeling in achieving self-love is joy. What comes to mind or what feeling do you experience when you hear the word joy? Is it a specific person or event, such as Christmas or Hanukah as a child, your children embracing you and telling you that they love you? Is it a man or woman at your work or you follow on social media or your spouse that always inspires you and sprinkles joy all around? For me, joy is sparked by the love of what my life is about—the people and things around me, family and the opportunity to help others achieve success and joy.

Drawing forth joy within yourself promotes healing and puts you on the path to creating self-love, Merriam Webster defines joy as:

a.   The emotion evoked by well-being, success, or good fortune or by the prospect of possessing what one desires: delight.

b.   The expression or exhibition of such emotion: gaiety.

c.   A state of happiness or felicity: bliss. source or cause of delight.

When joy is invoked, it results in love for yourself, others, your true calling and the environment around you.

So how can you get to that point? Well, the most important thing to do is to surround yourself with people and things that spark joy. There was a book on de-cluttering by Marie Kondo that speaks about only keeping items that spark joy inside you. Well, this rings true for creating self-love as well. The people you keep around you need to be ones that lift you up and spark joy in your heart. Always remember…it takes more than one spark to light a flame.

Place items in your home and work environment that truly spark joy, so when you walk into a room, you light up inside.

In my kitchen, the number of protein powders and supplements kept out on my counter made an area look cluttered and uninspiring, I finally decided that I would order canisters to put the powders in and make the kitchen light me up when I'm making breakfast and lunches in the morning. I splurged on Mackenzie Childs glass containers with black and white check lids and a red knob. They look awesome in my kitchen. It may seem simple, but it makes such a big impact on my day.

Affirmations are incredibly valuable as well. Early in my life, I used affirmations daily.

Here is how you create your affirmations. Come up with three or more adjectives of what you want to have in your life: I am a_____, _____, _____woman/man/leader (creating/attracting) _____ and _____ with ease and effortlessness. For example, "I am a powerful, courageous, loving woman attracting new business partners and customers daily with ease and effortlessness." Since I help create successful entrepreneurs growing an online business, that is a great affirmation for the results I want to create, and I always end with 'ease and effortlessness' because I think that is important. No one wants it to be difficult.

Keep in mind how much time you spend in doing things, going through the motions. What about those to-do lists that are filled with a constant flow of never-ending tasks? How many of us get to say at the end of the day that we accomplished every single item on those lists? Lastly and most importantly, did it matter?

As we hunt for joy and self-love, often times it looks more like seeking approval. Completing tasks just to get appreciation and acknowledgment from outside sources. I am absolutely guilty of that, it made me a highly competitive person and fed my need to win. However, winning never felt good because it was tied to something or someone showering me with praise for a job well done, and of course, if I won, I would be 'good enough'—for just a moment anyway.

Don't get me wrong, acknowledgment and praise feel good, and I am the first to give it, but when our lives become solely focused on 'doing', burnout, resentment, and fatigue can set in. Eventually, we feel of discouraged and disillusioned, which in turn affects our self-love and self-esteem. It is a vicious cycle that gets stopped in its tracks when you bring sparks of joy into your life.

When I reflect on my life now, I love, honor and respect myself, and I acknowledge myself for the difference I make in the people's lives. I get to be a cause, a source of power for creating self-love, joy and success all around me, every day because I choose being before doing. Each and every one of us has a gift that makes a difference somewhere and to someone.

My gift is vision and the ability to share and create a vision with others. I honor myself and my heart by choosing to share my gifts. As a result, I get to create and connect with joy daily.

A few years back, I worked in the mortgage industry. It was where I learned and developed myself as a success coach and mentor. I was very successful in the profession, and I had a killer life, and I am grateful for it. However, I was rarely present in my life or with the people around me. I was too busy thinking about how to keep it all together and how I may appear to others. I was as far as you could get from self-love. I was on the hamster wheel of what a successful career life appeared to be. It took me down the path of burnout, despair, and depression. My life was all about the results could I produce each day.

I would wake my kids up each morning and drive them to daycare and school, and then go to work. That evening I would then pick up the kids, come back home, feed them, bathe them, work some more, and then go to bed. Sound familiar? That was my life for many years, I was a great 'doer'. My family time was compromised, and even when I was spending time with them, I was too exhausted to really revel in the moments. I had anxiety about what could happen with my loans or clients rather than being at peace and 'being present' with my husband and children. My anxiety level was high, and I most certainly was not living by the tools I live by now.

After years of this crazy lifestyle, I knew I wanted something different. I craved it. I realized I needed to reinvent myself. I wanted to create different results for myself while continuing to help others at a high level. I had to design a new vehicle that would bring the income I envisioned, and the freedom to spend quality time with my family and friends. I needed to re-discover my passion and find joy again.

As my reinvention began, I had to really get clear and be brutally honest with myself on what I wanted my lifestyle to be like and not settle for anything less than the vision I created. I read books, studied, and took classes in everything from hypnosis and reiki to master business coaching. I peeled back layer after layer, diving in and really allowing myself to transform and blossom into the loving, joyful source of power and miracles I am today.

There was one last snippet of something that was holding me back. It was that one thing that is the hardest to let go of. Are you ready for it? Here it is; giving up caring what other people thought of me and being judged. This can be one of the toughest things as we live in a world of instant gratification where everyone appears perfect on social media...ha, what a joke!

The opportunity that I was embarking on was one that carried a lot of stigma in the past, but I crushed it and partnered with a marketing company. Guess what? My choice led me to a new level of self-love, enthusiasm, joy, and excitement. Once I made the decision to commit 100%, go all in and shook off the opinions of others, something big shifted in my life. I built a tribe of amazing people who wanted the same things I did: self-love, joy, success, time, and the financial freedom to do the things they wanted whenever they wanted.

I chose to fully experience this new vehicle, and I am inspired every single day. I share my joy and passion, tools, and strategies with hundreds of people every day. I am truly blessed and so very proud of my ever-growing team. My team members are inspired, enthusiastic and becoming powerhouse leaders filled with joy and drive.

Are you ready for the first key to creating self-love and the joy-filled life you love?

The first thing you must do when your eyes open in the morning is to affirm to yourself that you are happy, filled with joy, and are in great health. Follow with your desired results for that day. When I coach, I teach a visualization technique to use, and it's fabulous. Connect with me on social media and I will share it with you.

The second key to self-love requires an optimal environment for continued growth. Always read, listen to audiobooks, and go to live events. Continue to stretch yourself and peel back layer after layer, this will be a huge benefit to your self-love journey. There are many personal and professional development companies all over the world, and it's an incredible opportunity to make big strides with big transformations relatively quickly.

The third key is to 'be'. Answering the question at the beginning of this chapter, does it matter? Be joyful and inspirational, feed your mind and soul daily with positive content that aligns with your dreams and goals. If you are an unhappy 'do'er, what you are doing will not matter because it will never be enough. Your subconscious will seek out a match and hand you 'not enoughs', and your to-do list will be never-ending or fulfilling.

Lastly, the fourth key is to surround yourself with people who lift you up, who inspire you and make you rise. There is a saying that you become the average of the five people closest to you. If surround yourself with negative people who are stagnant in their life and find joy in gossiping about other people and putting their success down, then you will too. Hang out and work with people who have walked the path before you, who have achieved more than you and cause you to operate on a higher level. Then you will rise too. In addition, people who feel good about themselves will always produce bigger and better results. Find your tribe and love them. It is what I do with my team, we lock arms and work together. I teach them how to help others build tribes online, how to create and achieve their vision and dreams. It is a high-level vibe, and it feels good.

I want to leave you with another significant aspect of my reinvention: wake up with gratitude every morning. I still do this today. Every morning when I wake up (regardless of how well I have slept), the first thing I say to myself is, *I am happy, I am healthy, and attracting the best people for me into my life.* I add that I already have my desired goal in my life. I begin the day in a positive light. No negativity allowed.

I love myself today because I am what I do. I embody self-love and joy, and I create my day the way I want it to be. I choose to share my gifts with others. I help other people experience happy and full lives, creating wealth, abundance, and priceless time with their loved ones. It is possible to become successful inside and out and accomplish your highest goals and dreams. Be, then do, and you will have! If I can do it, you can do it too.

Lessons Learned and Mindset Tips

Lessons Learned:

1. Surround yourself with people who lift you up and inspire you. Be in action and be present to miracles all around you.

2. Always work on yourself. Take seminars, work with coaches, and continue your personal development journey.

3. You create life with your thoughts words, and actions. Eliminate thoughts that don't support your goals and dreams. Speak words that align with your goals and dreams and take inspired actions to achieve them. You truly are the source of your miracles, speak them into existence.

Mindset Tips:

1. Surround yourself with things that spark joy in your life. You will know it when you feel it because it lights you up inside. That goes for people and things, don't settle for cheap imitations. Go for the real deal.

2. When you wake up in the morning the first words you should say are, "I am happy, I am healthy, and I am (or have. Whatever your desire is)." Do this every morning until it becomes a habit and you do it without thinking about it

3. When self-doubt or fear sneaks in, immediately release it with three words: delete, delete, delete. Let it go and fill the blank space with, "I am happy, I am healthy, I am loved, I am worthy and deserving of my goals and dreams."

Aha Moments and Self-Reflections

Note your Thoughts

Conclusion

Your journey with us has come to an end…for now. We hope that you have discovered that we all can learn to love ourselves. *What's Self-Love Got To Do With It* is a timeless piece. You can be five or fifty-five years of age and still learn about self-worth and self-love.

I hope that what you have read between these pages has been insightful and helped guide you to understand more about the process of self-love and how important it is.

It is a journey of love, kindness, and understanding of self. It is a personal journey, not one size fits all description. It is about finding out what's working and not working for you. It is about being real with yourself and asking yourself some very pointed questions. It involves reworking schedules and digging into your heart and soul to ignite the fire that gets you out of bed in the morning. It's about looking at yourself in the mirror and knowing you are worthy and deserving of the life you want. It's about being open to receiving that life.

Open yourself up to the knowledge that there is a different path. It's about choice and understanding that although there may be obstacles in your path, there will also be unlimited opportunities. Self-discovery and self-love is a way of life, not a destination. There will be highs and lows but recognizing your love for yourself is the most important commodity you can have.

Our wish, as authors, is to inspire you to dig deep. Find your passion and purpose and have a love affair with yourself. The world is waiting for you. The path may not be easy, but I have learned that one of the best questions to ask is, "What am I to learn from this experience?" The lessons you learn along the way will be part of the journey to self-love.

The stories shared with you are raw and vulnerable, from the heart and soul of each author. With each chapter, we hope you learned new lessons and mindset tips that will allow you to reflect on your life through journaling in the notes pages.

A strong sense of self-worth and knowing what fuels you are the foundation for a successful life and business. You must feel worthy and ready to receive all the blessings you deserve. It took me several thousands of dollars to figure out what I already knew deep within myself. So, what is the answer to the burning question of what's self-love got to do with it? It is the essence of everything good in your life.

The world is shifting; women want the flexibility of working from home. This means more freedom, fun, and family stability. This is a paradigm shift and a movement to a new space.

We are all connected with communities wanting collaboration and calling to pay it forward.

It is said that when each of us shines our light, it gives permission for others to shine theirs.

Join us in our Facebook group where we come together to share about loving ourselves.
https://www.facebook.com/groups/whatsselflovegottodowithit/

After all the 'aha' moments and self-reflective journaling, my question for you is, are you ready to act? You have read it here. Action makes passion. It creates momentum.

A few questions you may want to ask yourself are:

1. Are you a busy entrepreneur who is not charging your full value?

2. Do you feel stuck in the chaotic spin of life?

3. Do you question whether you are worthy of the life you have dreamed of and not sure how to get there?

4. Are you maxed out? Do you see no end to the daily grind of work, kids, and activities?

How did this happen? How did you get so tired that you could question your self-worth and self-love?

You are not alone.

I encourage you to stop for a moment and think about the feelings that occurred as you read the stories in this book and reflected on your own lessons learned and mindset tips. If you find yourself saying, "This is too hard" or "I can't do it by myself," then my answer is that you are not meant to do it on your own.

As a lifestyle strategist, publisher, and having lived my own self-worth reinvention, I can tell you that there is a different way! There is a way for you to get a grip on the chaos, harness your energy and your self-worth and build your business without sacrificing yourself and your relationships. You can have all the love, laugh, serenity and business success. You can do it by asking for support from your loved ones or friends. It might even involve hiring a mentor or enrolling in a course. The choice is yours.

I have been where you are, and I understand. There is a different path for you.

Let's talk!

Heather Andrews
http://heatherandrews.press/group-coaching/

Do you dream of being a published author?

The best part of what I do is bringing people together to write, share, and inspire those that may feel alone or in need of healing. Your story could help to heal others.

My team will guide you through the writing process, so your idea can become a reality to be shared on worldwide distribution channels.

A book has been referenced as an authority piece for centuries and is known to be one of the best ways to gain instant credibility and visibility with clients in the online and offline space.

If you have a story to share and want to become a published author or co-author in a collaborative, then let's talk.

Email me at <u>heather@followitthru.com</u>

Here's to your story and someone waiting to read it.

Heather

CPSIA information can be obtained
at www.ICGtesting.com
Printed in the USA
BVHW08s0155290618

520318BV00010B/72/P